John Dune
January 15[^]
2002

Frank Gehry

Frank Gehry

The City and Music

Jeremy Gilbert-Rolfe with Frank Gehry

G+B ARTS INTERNATIONAL
Australia • Canada • France • Germany • India • Japan • Luxembourg
Malaysia • The Netherlands • Russia • Singapore • Switzerland

Copyright © 2001 OPA (Overseas Publishers Association) N.V. Published by license under the G+B Arts International imprint, part of The Gordon and Breach Publishing Group.

Amsteldijk 166
1st Floor
1079 LH Amsterdam
The Netherlands

British Library Cataloguing in Publication Data

A catalogue record for this book is available from the British Library.

ISBN: 90-5701-372-X

Cover   Frank Gehry & Associates: Walt Disney Concert Hall, Los Angeles, 1987–2003, final design model. Photo: Whit Preston, copyright FOG&A

For David Shapiro and Lindsey Stamm Shapiro

Contents

ix   Foreword

xi   List of Illustrations

xv   Acknowledgements

1   Introduction

13   Chapter 1
Improbable Logic

31   Chapter 2
Berlin: The Preservation of Insulation

63   Chapter 3
Los Angeles: Music and the Idea of the Centre

101   Chapter 4
Conclusion: The Practicality of Planes Taking Flight in Mass,
Towards Colour

129   Index

Foreword

I met Jeremy Gilbert-Rolfe at one of those informal New York soirées where a lot of important people meet to discuss a lot of important issues. I found Jeremy so matter-of-fact and refreshing that I stayed with him all evening, in the corner, talking about issues that were insignificant and exciting like 'where do you buy your shoes?' or 'you shouldn't smoke that much Jeremy' and 'isn't the vodka good?'. I was so intrigued by the guy that I wanted to see his paintings and to read his writings, both of which I pursued after that evening.

We got to know each other pretty well. We talked about art, we gossiped about our artist friends, he came to see my work, I went to see his work. I love his paintings. He's really cool. His intellect takes him to places in painting to which not many people go. I think he's very under-appreciated in that realm, but who am I to say?

The friendship led me to invite him to teach with me at Yale several times and to develop a combined course for the students in the architecture and art schools. The work that came out proved that there was a discussion possible between the two disciplines and the artists, strangely enough, succeeded in the architecture world. It was an exciting revelation for both Jeremy and myself. During the course of all of these encounters, and discussions about his painting, and discussions about my work, and discussion with the students, we developed a pretty solid understanding of what each of us was doing and why each was interested in the other's stuff.

This was why I was so excited by the idea of Jeremy doing this book. I can't put my finger on exactly how he understands what I'm doing, but I know he does. His writings here represent a point of view *vis-à-vis* my work that I don't think has been expressed elsewhere, and for that reason I find it very instructive, both in terms of what I'm doing now, and of what I hope to do in the future.

Jeremy listens hard to what I'm saying and takes seriously my ruminations. For example, in describing the Berlin Museum Island project, he clearly understood the political issues with which I was confronted, and how I was dealing with the practicalities of the project. He also understood the architectural ideas. The same was true of the Disney Concert Hall project; over time, he became intimately involved in the stormy seas in which that project floundered and resurfaced. He grasped the nuances of my architectural response to the problems, so that he was able to produce a clear and caring sort of report of what went on.

Jeremy has long understood—maybe even better than me—my own issues as 'architect-sculptor', which is a disconcerting area for me. I always thought that architecture was, by definition, a three-dimensional object and therefore sculpture. It is not quite that simple. Jeremy and I have discussed this many times and he has helped clarify some of those issues for me.

He also understands the relationship between programme and building form; the way I design very close to the bone of the programme, responding to the clients needs. He sees that my buildings are much more practical and carefully considered than they may seem at first view, and that this only unfolds to people after they use them. That was my game and Jeremy got it.

Frank Gehry

List of Illustrations

Fig. 1   Frank Gehry & Associates: Concord Pavillion, Concord, Californian, 1974–1977 (renovated 1994–1996). Photo: Morley Baer 1977

Fig. 2   Frank Gehry & Associates: American Center, Paris, 1988–1994. Photo: Erich Ansel Koyama 1974

Fig. 3   Frank Gehry & Associates: American Center, Paris, 1988–1994. Photo: Erich Ansel Koyama 1974

Fig. 4   Frank Gehry & Associates: Experience Music Project, Seattle, 1995–2000, design process model. Photo: Joshua White, 1997 Copyright FOG&A

Fig. 5   Frank Gehry & Associates: Experience Music Project, Seattle, 1995–2000, design process model. Photo: Joshua White, 1997 Copyright FOG&A

Fig. 6   Frank Gehry & Associates: Museum Island, Berlin, competition model Phase One. Photo: Joshua White, 1994 Copyright FOG&A

Fig. 7   Frank Gehry & Associates: Museum Island, Berlin, competition model (drawing). Phase One Photo: Joshua White, 1994 Copyright FOG&A

Fig. 8   Frank Gehry & Associates: Museum Island, Berlin, competition model Phase One Photo: Joshua White, 1994 Copyright FOG&A

Fig. 9   Frank Gehry & Associates: Museum Island, Berlin, competition model Phase One Photo: Joshua White, 1994 Copyright FOG&A

Fig. 10   Frank Gehry & Associates: Museum Island, Berlin, competition model Phase One Photo: Joshua White, 1994 Copyright FOG&A

Fig. 11   Frank Gehry & Associates: Museum Island, Berlin, competition model Phase One Photo: Joshua White, 1994 Copyright FOG&A

Fig. 12   Frank Gehry & Associates: Museum Island, Berlin, competition model Phase One Photo: Joshua White, 1994 Copyright FOG&A

Fig. 13   Frank Gehry & Associates: Museum Island, Berlin, competition model Phase Two Photo: Joshua White, 1997 Copyright FOG&A

Fig. 14   Frank Gehry & Associates: Museum island, Berlin, competition model Phase Two Photo: Joshua White, 1997 Copyright FOG&A

Fig. 15   Frederich Stüler: Neues Museum, 1843–1859, Museum Island, Berlin

Fig. 16   Frank Gehry & Associates: Museum Island, Berlin, competition model Phase Three Photo: Joshua White, 1997 Copyright FOG&A

Fig. 17   Frank Gehry & Associates: Museum Island, Berlin, competition model Phase Three Photo: Joshua White, 1997 Copyright FOG&A

Fig. 18 Frank Gehry & Associates: Museum Island, Berlin, competition model Phase One Photo: Joshua White, 1994 Copyright FOG&A

Fig. 19 Frank Gehry & Associates: Museum Island, Berlin, competition model Phase One Photo: Joshua White, 1994 Copyright FOG&A

Fig. 20 (top) Frank Gehry & Associates: Walt Disney Concert Hall, Los Angeles, 1987–2003, design process model Photo: Joshua White, 1993 Copyright FOG&A

Fig. 21 Frank Gehry & Associates: Walt Disney Concert Hall, Los Angeles, 1987–2003, design process model Photo: Joshua White, 1993 Copyright FOG&A

Fig. 22 Frank Gehry & Associates: Walt Disney Concert Hall, Los Angeles, 1987–2003, competition model. Photo: Tom Bonner, 1988 Copyright FOG&A

Fig. 23 Frank Gehry & Associates: Walt Disney Concert Hall, Los Angeles, 1987–2003, design process model Photo: Brian Yoo, 1991 Copyright FOG&A

Fig. 24 (top) Frank Gehry & Associates: Walt Disney Concert Hall, Los Angeles, 1987–2003, design process model Photo: Brian Yoo, 1991 Copyright FOG&A

Fig. 25 Frank Gehry & Associates: Walt Disney Concert Hall, Los Angeles, 1987–2003, competition model Photo: Tom Bonner, 1988 Copyright FOG&A

Fig. 26 Frank Gehry & Associates: Walt Disney Concert Hall, Los Angeles, 1987–2003, competition model Photo: Tom Bonner, 1988 Copyright FOG&A

Fig. 27 Frank Gehry & Associates: Walt Disney Concert Hall, Los Angeles, 1987–2003, competition model Photo: Tom Bonner, 1988 Copyright FOG&A

Fig. 28 Frank Gehry & Associates: Walt Disney Concert Hall, Los Angeles, 1987–2003, competition model Photo: Tom Bonner, 1988 Copyright FOG&A

Fig. 29 Frank Gehry & Associates: Walt Disney Concert Hall, Los Angeles, 1987–2003, competition model Photo: Tom Bonner, 1988 Copyright FOG&A

Fig. 30 Frank Gehry & Associates: Walt Disney Concert Hall, Los Angeles, 1987–2003, final design model Photo: Whit Preston, 1999 Copyright FOG&A

Fig. 31 Frank Gehry & Associates: Walt Disney Concert Hall, Los Angeles, 1987–2003, final design model Photo: Whit Preston, 1999 Copyright FOG&A

Fig. 32 Frank Gehry & Associates: Walt Disney Concert Hall, Los Angeles, 1987–2003, final design model Photo: Whit Preston, 1999 Copyright FOG&A

Fig. 33 Frank Gehry & Associates: Walt Disney Concert Hall,

Los Angeles, 1987–2003, final design model Photo: Whit Preston, 1999 Copyright FOG&A

Fig. 34 Frank Gehry & Associates: Walt Disney Concert Hall, Los Angeles,1987–2003, final design model Photo: Whit Preston, 1999 Copyright FOG&A

Fig. 35 Frank Gehry & Associates: Nationale Nederlanden Bank Building, Prague, 1992–1996, Photo: Mark Salette, 1997 Copyright FOG&A

Fig. 36 Frank Gehry & Associates: Walt Disney Concert Hall, Los Angeles, 1987–2003, final design model Photo: Whit Preston, 1999 Copyright FOG&A

Fig. 37 Frank Gehry & Associates: Guggenheim Museum, Bilbao, 1991–1997. Photo: David Heald Copyright SRDF, NY, 1997

Fig. 38 Frank Gehry & Associates: Guggenheim Museum, Bilbao, 1991–1997. Photo: David Heald Copyright SRDF, NY, 1997

Fig. 39 Frank Gehry & Associates: Guggenheim Museum, Bilbao, 1991–1997. Photo: David Heald Copyright SRDF, NY, 1997

Fig. 40 Frank Gehry & Associates: Guggenheim Museum, Bilbao, 1991–1997. Photo: David Heald Copyright SRDF, NY, 1997

Fig. 41 Frank Gehry & Associates: Guggenheim Museum, Bilbao, 1991–1997. Photo: David Heald Copyright SRDF, NY, 1997

Fig. 42 Frank Gehry & Associates: Guggenheim Museum, Bilbao, 1991–1997. Photo Copyright: Christian Richters, 1997

Fig. 43 Frank Gehry & Associates: Guggenheim Museum, Bilbao, 1991–1997. Photo: David Heald Copyright SRDF, NY, 1997

Fig. 44 Frank Gehry & Associates: Guggenheim Museum, Bilbao, 1991–1997. Photo Copyright: Christian Richters, 1997

Fig. 45 Frank Gehry & Associates: Guggenheim Museum, Bilbao, 1991–1997. Photo: David Heald Copyright SRDF, NY, 1997

Fig. 46 Frank Gehry & Associates: Guggenheim Museum, Bilbao, 1991–1997. Photo Copyright: Jeff Goldberg/Esto, 1997

Fig. 47 Frank Gehry & Associates: Neue Zollhof, Dusseldorf, 1995–1999, final design model Photo: Whit Preston, 1999 Copyright FOG&A

Fig. 48 Frank Gehry & Associates: Neue Zollhof, Dusseldorf, 1995–1999, final design model Photo: Whit Preston, 1999 Copyright FOG&A

Fig. 49 Frank Gehry & Associates: Neue Zollhof, Dusseldorf, 1995–1999. Photo: Tomaso Bradshaw, 1997 Copyright FOG&A

Fig. 50 Frank Gehry & Associates: Neue Zollhof, Dusseldorf, 1995–1999. Photo: Tomaso Bradshaw, 1997 Copyright FOG&A

Fig. 51 Frank Gehry & Associates: Neue Zollhof, Dusseldorf, 1995–1999. Photo: Tomaso Bradshaw, 1998 Copyright FOG&A

Fig. 52 Frank Gehry & Associates: Neue Zollhof, Dusseldorf, 1995–1999. Photo: Tomaso Bradshaw, 1997 Copyright FOG&A

Fig. 53 Frank Gehry & Associates: Neue Zollhof, Dusseldorf, 1995–
1999. Photo: Tomaso Bradshaw, 1998 Copyright FOG&A

Fig. 54 Frank Gehry & Associates: Neue Zollhof, Dusseldorf, 1995–
1999. Window Study Photo: Joshua White, 1996 Copyright
FOG&A

Fig. 55 Frank Gehry & Associates: Stata Center, MIT, Cambridge, Mass.,
1998–2004, final design model, Photo: Whit Preston, 2000
Copyright FOG&A

Fig. 56 Frank Gehry & Associates: Stata Center, MIT, Cambridge, Mass.,
1998–2004, final design model, Photo: Whit Preston, 2000
Copyright FOG&A

Fig. 57 Frank Gehry & Associates: Guggenheim Museum, Bilbao,
1991–1997 Photo: David Heald Copyright SRDF, NY, 1997

Fig. 58 Frank Gehry & Associates: Walt Disney Concert Hall,
Los Angeles, 1997–2003, final design model. Photo:
Whit Preston, 1999 Copyright FOG&A

Acknowledgements

This book would not have been written had Frank Gehry not been patiently prepared to address any question I asked, regardless of whether it was interesting or not. I must also thank Kurt W Forster, for conversations we have had about architecture in general, as well as those about Frank's work in particular, and Dietrich Wildung for kindly responding to some questions raised by his essay, quoted here. I should also mention the usefulness to me of remarks made over the years about Frank's work by my wife, Genevieve Gilbert-Rolfe, and John Johnston and Joe Masheck. More practically, this book could not have been written without Chris Herlinger and Keith Mendenhall, of Frank O Gehry and Associates, who made it possible for Frank and me to meet and who provided the documentation we required, and my assistant Gabrielle Jennings, who proof-read earlier drafts of the manuscript and helped with much else. I am indebted to them and to Melissa Larner, who in editing the manuscript made a large number of suggestions that caused me to improve it, and, last but not least, to Diana Thater for the index.

INTRODUCTION

This book began as an enquiry into all the buildings that Frank Gehry had proposed but was unable to build, and the various reasons for this. It soon came to focus on the reformulation of Berlin's Museum Island complex (the first round of the competition for which began in 1994) and the Disney Concert Hall in Los Angeles. The latter is now to be built after all—its completion date as we go to press, 2003—while the former remains a missed opportunity. Both are architectural programmes concerned with how bodies occupy not dwelling spaces, but public spaces in which things or experiences are temporarily dwelt *on*—in the museum by walking around and in the concert hall by sitting still. Focusing on them has allowed me to concentrate, in turn, on the two questions about Gehry's work that I find most engaging: what he thinks cities are and need, and the musicality through which his buildings defeat stasis and reintroduce the phenomenal space of the body to architecture.

Gehry is surely right to say that the idea of 'truth to materials' is silly in an age when one can build anything one can draw, and it may therefore be more fruitful to think instead about truth to ideas, in the sense in which Leonardo da Vinci said the idea was in the drawing. However, in Gehry's work the drawing is often about movements as much as forms. Chapter 1 expands on the Introduction to describe in general terms the movements Gehry's programmes associate with architecture. These are bodily, sculptural, socio- and techno-cultural, drawn out of the materials, the site and the surrounding landscape. Chapter 2 discusses the Museum Island project in Berlin primarily as movements that would have united the museums with one another but also with the city (setting them apart from, but as a part of, it). Chapter 3 discusses movement in the Disney Concert Hall as a preparation for a transference of attention from looking to listening. Chapter 4 examines its use in the Bilbao Guggenheim as a defamiliarisation of the visual as it is normally encountered, which prepares the viewer for works of visual art.

Departing from the stability of the brick and the post and lintel in favour of structures more involved with an idea of movement, Gehry's buildings look unusual in part because of their practicality, but equally—to borrow a phrase from the sculptor Sol Lewitt—because he doesn't want to make things he's seen before. The interrelationship between democracy in the programme and movement in the form—two themes important to Gehry, which will recur here—is to be found in the way in which his buildings are comfortable while at the same time challenging to the perception and imagination.

If Gehry has learned from Los Angeles, where he grew up and has always worked, perhaps what he has learned appears in his architecture as an understanding of the specifically contemporary relationship between mobility and deorigination that living there suggests. The great distances of Los Angeles County are populated by individual automotive units communicating by mobile phone while in constant movement, placelessness a condition of the place, time unrelated to space. Gehry's development has comparably involved him in the rediscovery of the spatial in relation to a sense of time as much technological as it is organic, and in which there is no necessary relationship between proximity and immediacy. As to the deoriginated, it is that which, unexpectedly, has found a way to live without its putative origins in the sense of being outside them: it thinks not through, but about and with them, from elsewhere.

In the 1980s, Gehry's work was discussed in the light of an application of deconstruction to architecture, which seemed to boil down to a kind of formalism that required the building to be made out of defamiliarised architectural conventions. That is not the kind of deconstructive impulse with which one wants to associate deorigination (in which deconstruction is as it were grounded or originated) here. This is because in Gehry's work the site, the language of architecture, and the materials it employs, are deoriginated through a process that is not motivated or characterised by a rhetoric of negation and subversion, ie, which is not critically motivated. Nothing that bears on the intrinsic shape of the building is the product of a critical impulse except in the sense in which the work of art always is—wrenching apart the idea of art so that it may remake it. On the contrary, it is a process of imagining and revising that depends on a familiar, Kantian, idea of intuition through which it seeks to locate the meaning of the building in the visual as presence rather than referent. Gehry's approach is not speculative in the sense that David Goldblatt has said that Peter Eisenman's architecture, 'like the collected works of other postmodernists, is less interested in providing answers to questions (eg, what is a church? what is a bookstore? a home?) than in generating questions, conversations, about what such questions might mean and in what new ways they might be approached'.[1] Gehry answers rather than asks those questions—not least during conversation about them with the client. The building's shape follows from the programme and its realisation through a manipulation of materials that need not be true to them, ie, deoriginates them almost before it starts. His architecture is not so much about making one wonder what the meaning of a functional denotation may ultimately be, as what it is like to be in this particular building. And that is intended to give way, when appropriate, to what one is there to do. Gehry doesn't want to problematise the museum so much as he wants to build a better museum. He doesn't want you to think about what a museum is when you're trying to look at a work of art. Practicality aside, the difference is one of enjoyment of an affirmative rather than a critical sort.

Counter-critical, Gehry's buildings excite in the way that Matisse is exciting. They provoke their detractors all the more because theirs is a provocation delivered through the medium of the pleasurable rather than the didactic (which, in being serious, eschews pleasure save for the pleasure of pure reason—pleasure without the body, which is its source). They are democratic in this too, providing access without requiring an appreciation grounded in recognising that a critical act of some laudatory sort has taken place. Their form is often that of an elaborated cube, freed by its elaboration from modernist architecture's inherently classical predilection for an image of integrity based on the idea of the whole and its subdivision. In that respect, they are able to propose a mobile relationship between surface and structure that leads to a more complex elaboration of mobility as a property or quality of contemporary life or thinking. The implications of this also return one to the theme of the democratic.

It may be because Gehry (like Jacques Derrida) does not regard architecture as an ultimately critical act—while Eisenman may have committed himself to the (potentially incoherent) proposal that it should be fundamentally nothing else—that Gehry has been able to move beyond his earlier work, which could more readily, if inaccurately, be seen as defamiliarisation with critical intent. Gehry's architecture began with slicing into forms and has become a practice of extending and adding onto them, so that one may say that his architecture began with a kind of defamiliarisation reminiscent of Viktor Shklovsky's notion of the laying bare of the device, but has since turned into an architecture of deferral and flow, suggesting post-Structuralism rather than Russian Formalism.

Discussing Gehry's later work as an architecture of deferral and flow leads to an inverted Heidegger—one at home in the ungrounded, where its relationship to its context is concerned—but to (an uninverted) Kant in its exploration of its intrinsics—and, I shall say in Chapter 3, in another direction, towards Gilles Deleuze. It is not possible to return the programme to the site as Heidegger would have wished, and the building is integrated into its context both by acknowledging it and standing apart from it—but that is not to say that the way it acknowledges it is the same way it stands apart. If there is an idea that unites Gehry's buildings with their locales and vice versa it is that there is more than one idea in play at any single place or time. In the sense that he adapts the programme—considered as an array of materials and processes—to the site in such a way as to make it impossible to say with any kind of certainty what comes first, his work is perhaps best described in terms of a dynamic parallelism. On the one hand, the programme's requirements as a function of the site and the same programme as stimulus for a visual idea on the other—a relocated hermeneutics in parallel with an unreconstructed intuition.

Kant related aesthetic experience to making the 'life force', as he called it, present to cognition, which is to say, *re*presented, in some way—hence Heidegger's indebtedness to, and need to rethink, him. Any building would be obliged to refer—if only involuntarily through its interposition in it—to its site as a specific place serving a general, and therefore siteless (to the extent that it is universal), function. What goes on in the buildings discussed here could after all happen anywhere, in the sense that the arts are performed everywhere. The building enables a universal function to take place at a particular spot on the globe. It is in what happens as Gehry makes the intrinsics of the building reinvent its context, once at the level of its relationship to its physical environment, and once as an expression of the programme, in a way that allows the building to stand apart as a kind of sculptural entity from what it otherwise reformulates and subsumes, that one may want to say—in what seems like paradox but is not—in Gehry's work, singularity is a product of the universal.

The terms of that singularity relate to another question about Gehry's relationship to the contemporary, which has to do with whether, as one writer has said, the essence of the contemporary is its unrepresentability.[2] The reverse would seem to be more obviously true. If the contemporary has an essence, it is that it knows itself as infinite representation. If the contemporary resists representation, this is because it is always representing itself to itself, ie, it is presentation rather than representation that eludes it, and it is not clear to me that resistance has anything to do with it. The electronic communication characteristic of the contemporary is only ever present as representation, while being experienced as more immediate or real than the actuality it parallels. It is against this background that Gehry uses familiar materials to reformulate that which can only represent because of its familiarity—the familiar is re-presentation by definition—by making them behave differently, and therefore to do something for the first time to the language of re-presentation in which the contemporary is lodged. This can begin as a simple reversal through which Gehry can exploit a material's latent potential for self-contradiction. For example, in earlier works such as his own house (1978) and the Santa Monica Place Mall (1973/1980), he made wire mesh stand for openness and penetration rather than exclusion and confinement. In doing so, he turned its associations back on themselves, neutralising its familiar associations by reversing them, while simultaneously, in its continuing to serve as divider and limit, retaining their usual iconic meaning. He turns this tendency back on itself to make the iconic become the material of a form. This simultaneous cancelling and invoking of the familiar is, however, only the first of a two-stage process. The second follows from the destabilisation of fixed iconic meaning. The building takes ambiguously from both sides of the equation—wire mesh is still a cheap and familiar material, but because of Gehry's reversal of some of its associations, it behaves in a manner quite unlike itself—exhausting or overcomplicating the iconic in an excess of representation that is either accompanied by, or is possibly what drives one's attention to, presentation. Referentiality having thus been at once saturated and drained, Gehry is free to engage one's sense of wire mesh's physical characteristics. Which is to say, of their (phenomenal) presence as once latent but now apparent visual effects—having to do with the colour of wire mesh, its being metal present as a web rather than a slab, etc—which are now part of an architectural event.[3]

Gehry himself is quick to attribute much of his thinking to contemporary artists, particularly to American sculptors of the 1960s, with two of whom especially—Claes Oldenberg and Richard Serra—he has a long history of collaboration. Running before or below his interest in the work of individual artists, there is the possibility that he saw in 1960s sculpture a potential for rethinking architecture that followed from sculpture's origin as architectural supplement. The Renaissance description of sculpture as a homeless art, existing to link the conceptual space of painting with the real space of architecture, fits most of the sculpture of the 1960s. It described itself as 'fac[ing] problems such as the material's integrity, gravity, time, site, and dimension',[4] and it seems significant that it frequently used materials reminiscent of experiences connected with buildings. The artists themselves though, tended at the time to want to disassociate their own work from its debt to architecture and especially from the possibility that it could remind one of architecture. To this day it remains odd to me that many writers describe Gehry's architecture as sculptural, but there is little written about Minimalism as architectural, which I think is a result of that movement's insistence that 'The art of the late 1960s marked the end of symbolism'.[5]

For example, when I first arrived in New York, at the end of the 1960s, people would become cross if one described Donald Judd's sculpture as a rearrangement of elements in the architectural environment recalling either buildings under construction, in its use of plywood, or the stainless steel and Plexiglas elevators in fancy skyscrapers. (Now the observation would be less controversial.) Moreover, in addition to the materials it used—and not only because it was a movement doctrinally opposed to painting, although that is of defining importance—the form of Minimalist sculpture, particularly of the first generation, was explicitly architectonic in a number of respects. It was geometric rather than organic. It was hollow (Judd, Robert Morris) rather than carved or axially articulated, animating space through the idea of the container (a box in Judd and Morris, an open and permeable grid in Sol Lewitt) rather than the figure or the field. It foregrounded construction and physically apprehensible stress. Ronald Bladen and Robert Grosvenor's work from the 1960s, and in a related but different way, Carl Andre's early work, represent this most fully, while second-generation Minimalism sees Andre's version of the Minimalist idea taken to a further condition of provisionality rather than fixity in Serra's *One Ton Prop (House of Cards)* (1969). It sought to share a space with the viewer with the immediacy that buildings do, as opposed to words or pictures traditionally conceived (ie, requiring recognition and interpretation before they can be felt). In its fundamentalist desire to overcome the pictorial, for which it insisted on preserving the most traditional definition available, Minimalism sought the look of the impersonal rather than the personal, the industrial rather than the handmade, which one associates with buildings rather than paintings. One could say then that it was a sculptural movement driven back to architecture by virtue of the materials it used and because it was anti-pictorial.

This dependence on architecture as model and material resource causes me to wonder whether 1960s sculpture represented to Gehry something like architectural thinking in one sense freed from an architectural programme but in another longing for one. It may have been its hostility to the pictorial that drove 1960s sculpture towards architecture, but in the absence of an architectural programme, there is nothing for such sculpture to do but be in the way, orienting one to a view—an implicitly pictorial function—that it in fact impedes.

That is not what Gehry says, however. He says that 1960s sculpture just seemed to him to be more direct and adventurous than most of the architecture contemporaneous with it. This would not necessarily mean that its being direct and adventurous with architectural materials and terms was irrelevant. It may, however, explain why, whatever he got from them, Gehry seems never to have been prone to the certainties that became so debilitating to the sculptors of the 1960s: a reductivist idea of art and art history; faith in the modular; and (a much later development, reflecting a general shift in critical discourse) a passive-aggressive desire to preserve the monument in the anti-monumental. What he shares with it is above all the insistence on phenomenal presence as an uncontrollable bodily effect realised by Serra's best work, and the enlivening of space through playfulness combined with concentration seen in Oldenberg's. But Gehry's work exceeds the Minimalist aesthetic (as it also goes beyond Pop art's dependence on the icon while sharing with it an interest in making the familiar fresh). Gehry's work preserves and articulates tangibility through playfulness in a world where nearly everything else aspires to the intangible status of the sign—to being read rather than seen—and is better described in terms of an erotics than of a sculptural theory founded in the material's integrity, gravity, etc. For these reasons and others to which they give rise, the characterisation of sculpture as form engaged in activity offered by Gilles Deleuze and Félix Guattari is a better description of the constituents of Gehry's architecture than any that one might derive from Minimalism, precisely because they see sculpture in terms of movements:

> If methods are very different, not only in the different arts but in different artists, we can nevertheless characterise some great monumental types, or 'varieties' of compounds of sensations: *the vibration*, which characterises the simple sensation (but it is already durable or compound, because it rises and falls, implies a constitutive difference of level, follows an invisible thread that is more nervous than cerebral); *the embrace or the clinch* (when two sensations resonate in

each other by embracing each other so tightly in a clinch of what are no more than 'energies'); *withdrawal, sensation, distension* (when, on the contrary, two sensations draw apart, release themselves, but so as now to be brought together by the light, the air, or the void that sinks between them or into them, like a wedge that is at once so dense and so light that it extends in every direction as the distance grows, and forms a bloc that no longer needs a support). Vibrating sensation—coupling sensation—opening or splitting, hollowing out sensation. These types are displayed almost in their pure state in sculpture, with its sensations of stone, marble, or metal, which vibrate according to the order of strong or weak beats, projections and hollows, its powerful clinches that intertwine them, its development of large spaces between groups or within a single group where we no longer know whether it is the light or the air that sculpts or is sculpted.[6]

As the preface to this book attests, Gehry is very generous and seems not to notice that he improves, rather than simply reapplying, ideas to which he is attracted. He once described John Altoon's art to me as being like a fist, and has said of his first encounter with Serra's work that: 'His sculpture was raw and powerful, emotional and threatening—and minimal. Here was a guy who was pushing building-scale stuff around, and he got the most effect with the fewest number of moves'.[7] All of these properties are transformed rather than maintained in Gehry's work. Serra's aesthetic limits him to works in which very heavy planes are held up by themselves or by one another to form an image of the precarious in which gravity and what may defy it are locked in a condition of suspense. Gehry, having found in Minimalism new ways of getting the maximum effect with the fewest moves, has converted its language (back) into an architectural one in which everything that in sculpture had to be heavy may now be light, and where, in consequence, elaborate and varied movement has grown out of a rhetoric of the assertively reductive. A fist is not a complex sign or gesture. Gehry's work is powerful and emotional, but in it the raw is reworked into a symphonic complexity that has no interest in being threatening, because it is not sculpture but architecture. Also, I think, because his work is assertive but never grounded in negation.

Contemporary sculpture and Deleuze will reappear in the following pages. As will the sense in which Gehry's career has been inflected by Los Angeles. This is a city that also 'extends in every direction as the distance grows' and, as a rhizomic order of suburban enclaves seeking to evade urbanism, aims to form, and in some respects has succeeded in becoming, 'a bloc which no longer needs a support'. This is true at least inasmuch as no one leaves these suburbs except to go to another one and the centre exists only as that which one lives by avoiding.[8] Working in Los Angeles led Gehry to be more adventurous with materials than he might have been elsewhere.

At the same time, being in Venice or Santa Monica has meant that he wasn't in Manhattan, and this too may have had consequences. There are, for example, Gehry buildings in Berlin, Paris, and Prague, in Japan and South Korea, and in every other region of the United States, but as yet, nothing built from scratch in New York City. Though there are signs that this will change, if it does, the question of why it took so long will remain, and among the answers to it, his identification with southern California must be one reason.

There are two senses in which southern California encourages innovation in building methodology. It never rains, so having to withstand severe weather is not the kind of fundamental consideration it is elsewhere, and it has earthquakes. Gehry's use of a variety of materials to clad his buildings is a direct product of the Los Angeles building code, which requires external surfaces—stone, brick, or anything else—to hang off a screen. The weather may be predictable but the earth itself is not (which invites one to think of California as a benign Kantian landscape with a malignant Heideggerian ground, the reverse of the irreducibly secure—nature as Heidegger's revenge).

There is another regional characteristic that seems to have affected Gehry's aesthetic. This has to do with the quality of lightness, a condition at once natural and cultural in southern California. Southern California is indeed filled with light, looking much of the time like a large version of Provence in the same way that Virginia resembles an inflated Kent. But, as noted, southern California is also the home of impermanence as a virtue. When one alights from an aircraft in Los Angeles, one is at once struck with the light-filled quality of all that one sees. Unlike New York, London or Berlin, which impress one with that solidity possessed by stone and brick when they really are holding things up, Los Angeles presents itself as a movie image. Knowing it already on film, one's first encounter with it is a confirmation of a lifetime's cinematic experiences rather than an encounter with a new place.

Downtown Los Angeles, for example, precedes the earthquake laws and has stone buildings like that which houses the *Los Angeles Times*, but is so familiar from the noir films of the 1950s, it is possible that it never actually achieves physical substance in anyone's perception, for there can be few in Los Angeles who have never seen a 1950s crime movie. But it is also because the town is largely made of things that aren't meant to last. In this respect, and because it is the capital city of film, it is more at home in the twenty-first century than other cities, which pine for the nineteenth—or in the case of Berlin, the eighteenth. This is because, as both cinema and architecture—and above all, fashion—tell us, while portly meant substantial in the nineteenth century, thin meant successful in the twentieth. The great steel and stone buildings that celebrated capitalism during its heroic phase were made in the twentieth century of glass on a steel frame, a triumph of the light over the massive—and, therefore, potentially of the mobile over the slow or inert—and also of transparency over the idea of an ultimately inaccessible interior. Where banks used to bury money in a subterranean vault, they now put the safe in the window. No city could be said to be more responsive to the actual look of the culture at large than Los Angeles because that is its commercial life, Hollywood being to Los Angeles what Wall Street is to New York: the one a city of images, the other of numbers. This seems relevant to Gehry's architecture in that his buildings often appear to share in that capacity to attribute to things the lightness of an image that is characteristic of Los Angeles.

It is a lightness that follows from the ubiquity in Los Angeles of the principle that all reality is an image before it is a thing. The real can only simulate the image, by which it has always already been overpowered—as in Oscar Wilde's example of a sunset impersonating a Turner—because, as Jean Baudrillard has explained, images only simulate simulation, pretending to represent that on which they have already imposed new (their own) laws.[9] This is, *pace* Baudrillard, true of all human and post-human life under late capitalism, but in Los Angeles it is an explicit rather than implicit condition of everyday life, and may have helped Gehry to pursue the plastic possibilities of any given architectural programme further and sooner than he might have elsewhere. This is not because he is prepared in any way to sacrifice the function of the building to some interesting idea about aesthetic experience—putting a pole in the middle of a room, that sort of thing—but because he has been able to explore shape in a way that might have been harder outside an environment where it is presumed that the point of a building will be to distinguish itself from those around it, to offer itself as a unique image. As buildings in London and elsewhere cease to be rectilinear, causing scandal in the process, they recall Los Angeles, where Disney's Chief Executive is ensconced in a building shaped like the top of Mickey Mouse's head.

And this, of course, goes directly to another theme that concerns us here. To be reminded of Los Angeles when in London or Berlin is only to recognise with a particular severity that the age of things is past and that of the image well advanced. If truth to materials becomes fatuous when one can make materials do anything one wants, then meaning must lie in the disposition rather than the disposed, in the image rather than the thing. It is not that Los Angeles is taking over the world, as Gehry's European detractors protest; it's that Los Angeles has in this respect anticipated the world. One is merely experiencing the triumph of the sign that one sees everywhere in contemporary life, and which is characteristic of capitalism, particularly in its developed form. Los Angeles is one of its most developed forms, and as the sign globally replaces its referent, the world's cities come to look like Los Angeles—which had previously been a place in which there was an industry that, as the cinematic need arose, could replicate for reproduction on film any of those cities. The dilemma faced by nineteenth-century cities is not properly described as a struggle between their identities and a foreign version of themselves, but as a conflict between their past and the present.

Gehry's detractors are wrong in an important sense. His relationship to the socio-cultural generality is interesting because of the way in which he turns into form what the world gives him as a sign for itself. This should preclude him from being described as merely historically symptomatic—let alone an ardent representative—of an untransformed version of what he transforms. Gehry developed his aesthetic out of a knowledge that one could make contemporary materials do anything. The weather in Los Angeles made it possible for him to be more experimental in this regard, while the general absence of nineteenth-century stolidity encouraged experimentalism in every other respect. It is in his handling of practicalities such as these—and their development in the course of a passage from an earlier approach that involved slicing into a form to the current phase, which is more about elaborating a skin as an ectoplasm—that the political as well as the poetical dimension of Gehry's work is to be found. In Gehry's practice, the passage from interior to exterior structure has also been one of movement intensified at the expense of explicit references to stability. He has progressively displaced the modernist (and by parasitic or reactive default, postmodernist) foregrounding of the idea (always one in which structure stands for more structure, architecture as epistemology or iconography), replacing it with an elaboration of the event it facilitates—the conceptual ground subsumed and reimagined by perceived activity. The city and music—parallel orders with a shared interest in movement—provide the language and images through which this reimagining takes place.

Notes

1   David Goldblatt, 'ARCHITECTURE: Modernism to Postmodernism', *Oxford Encyclopedia of Aesthetics*, Oxford University Press, Oxford, 1998, p 94.
2   Mark Lilla, 'Pseud's Skyscraper', *London Review of Books*, 5 June 1997, p 33. (A review of Karsten Harries' *The Ethical Function of Architecture*, a book that will be cited extensively here, Lilla's is a good representative of a certain kind of essay about architecture that doesn't want it to be what it says it is but won't let it be anything else.)
3   Frederic Jameson sees the house as a combination of first- and third-world iconography, where wire mesh is always about the latter—ie, cheap, provisional, temporary, all that stone is not. In doing so, he is refusing to see it as something that could happen to him as opposed to being (in this case and in consequence mis-) interpreted by him. Frederic Jameson, *Postmodernism, or, The Cultural Logic of Late Capitalism* Duke University Press, Durham, North Carolina, 1991,

pp 108–129. Originally published as 'Spatial Equivalents: Postmodernist Architecture and the World System', in David Carrol (ed) *The States of Theory,* Columbia University Press, New York, 1990, pp 125–48. For a detailed rebuttal of Jameson's argument, see John H. Johnston 'Jameson's Hyperspace, Heidegger's Rift, Frank Gehry's House', in *America's Modernisms: Revaluing the Canon*, eds Kathryne V. Lindberg and Kranick, J.G. Louisiana State University Press, Baton Rouge and London, 1996, pp. 182–207.

4   Gregoire Müller, *The New Avant-Garde: Issues for the Art of the Seventies,* Praeger, New York, 1972, p 8.

5   Ibid.

6   Gilles Deleuze and Félix Guattari, *What is Philosophy?*, trans Graham Burchell and Hugh Tomlinson, Verso, London, 1994, p 168.

7   Joseph Giovannini, 'Bending Geometry, Two of a Kind', *The New York Times*, Sunday 29 August 1999, www.nytimes/qpass-archives.

8   See Jeremy Gilbert-Rolfe, *Beyond Piety; Essays in Art Criticism 1986–1993*, Cambridge University Press, New York, 1995, Chapter 35, 'Born to be Mild', pp 344–346.

9   Jean Baudrillard, *Simulations*, trans Paul Foss, Paul Patton and Philip Beitchman, Semiotext(e), New York, 1983, p 11.

CHAPTER 1
Improbable Logic

Peter Arnell: But you are an artist, right?

Frank Gehry: I'm an architect. I get that a lot because I've hung around with a lot of artists and I'm very close to a lot of them. I'm very involved in their work; I think a lot of my ideas have grown out of it, and that there's been some give and take. So sometimes I get called an artist. Somebody'll say, 'Oh, well, Frank's an artist'. I feel in a way that's used like a dismissal. I want to say I'm an architect. My intention is to make architecture.[1]

We were in Gehry's studio and he was talking about how successfully completing a project requires the architect to find solutions to all the things that go wrong, or become unexpectedly difficult, regardless of what they are. Gehry stopped in the middle of an anecdote that illustrated this point and smiled: 'But when it is built, and you see it for the first time with everything in it, it's as if an improbable event happens'.

I think it important that he uses the present tense rather than the past perfect because, generally speaking, what people seem either to like or dislike about Gehry's buildings is that they're active and imaginative—an event not a record. A Gehry building is the practical result and embodiment of a playful logic, found in the programme. The logic that Gehry finds in materials is also improbable: it does not follow from what a material is, but from what it might be used for, or become a part of. If the skyscraper is implicit in the steel frame, it is not similarly clear that the buildings discussed here are implicit in the materials out of which they are made.

They begin as paper models. 'Paper' says Gehry, 'is structure. If I can make it out of paper I know I can build it'. The question of what to build it from follows—of what a material might do if it were made to play a game for which it was not designed, of what logic might be found for it once its truth had become irrelevant. Kurt Forster, one of the first to explicate the body's role in Gehry's architecture, has said:

> I find it such an illustrative gesture, such a telling indication, that when he was given [some] Formica-like material, the first thing he did was to break it. To break something, to break away from its standard use, has an archaic, an almost childlike intensity about it—you break into it, you taste it, you sniff it, you take it apart, before you do something new to it.[2]

One could find in this a definition of the idea of truth to materials that would fit Gehry's work as the traditional one does not. Potentiality is a kind of truth, but one would have to give up on the idea of one true potential. Also, if one makes something do something it never did before, one is not misrepresenting it, although it may appear to have been led astray, or allowed to play. When people dislike Gehry's buildings, it is usually because they don't look like other buildings. It is there that their playfulness is most apparent, and therefore unsurprising that antipathy to their appearance is often explicitly linked to a desire to keep the present under control.

When you look at a Gehry building, you're looking at what contemporary life looks like when considered as a property of an architectural programme. The programme presents the present as containing the past while not—hence the threat of the uncontrollable—necessarily being continuous with it. It is even possible to say, necessarily not. Gehry's architecture playfully reimagines everything through an idea of the present as that which may not be brought fully under control, the contemporary as the unanticipated as well as the (whether dialectically or genealogically) predictable. Gehry wants his work to be playful in the way children are playful—which includes being inventively irresponsible with extant models—because he doesn't believe that the answers to an unanticipated present lie in a retrospective teleology imposed on the past. They lie as much, or more, in what separates the present from its precedents, in the sense of what has intervened between them, precluding the precedent from acting as a model for what comes after it.

This sense of the present as unanticipated, and in that respect as freeing one to play—indeed, obliging one to do so, since (of necessity) only inventiveness could provide a solution appropriate to a condition without recognisable precedent—inoculates Gehry against both the historicist and the futuristic. If the present is irreducible to its past, there is likewise no reason to suppose that the present may find either itself or what is to succeed it in the deployment of a symbolic futurity. As Gehry himself puts it, 'I think it's presumptuous to think you can build for the next century. I'm happy if I can just make it for the time I'm in.'[3]

Gehry's ideas about what might be done with, in, and for, the contemporary world by architecture are visible in the shape of his buildings, each of which mutate and develop in the course of a protracted engagement with the client, throughout which Gehry's mind is on how to activate the site. However, two themes in criticism of Gehry already introduced, and which will recur more than once in what follows, have in my opinion led to an underestimation of the poetic force unleashed by this practicality, one through overemphasis and the other through misunderstanding. An overemphasis on Gehry's relationship to sculpture has threatened to obscure the larger sense in which what the buildings look like follows from what they do. His playfulness, which could also simply be called 'inventiveness', is not critically driven in the sense that it seeks to take ideas from sculpture and use them to deconstruct architecture. In fact, his work is not critical in that sense at all. As noted, it does not start with negation and is not concerned with problematising institutional or epistemological categories. When Gehry uses wire mesh, that is neither a critique of the material, nor of the building in which he incorporates it. It is not about what the material isn't, but about what it can do. Its incorporation into the programme throws nothing into doubt except presumptions about what one can use in a building, and significantly, it is only there that one finds criticality in the work. However, this has not prevented those so inclined from seeing Gehry's architecture as exclusively critical. On occasion, this misunderstanding has been benevolent in motive and consequence—as when he received attention he might not otherwise have enjoyed during the deconstructive moment of the 1980s. But usually it is neither. Sometimes (as with the Museum Island in Berlin) it has been responsible for a misreading of the programme so total as to be dazzling were it not so depressing. It is a misunderstanding that Gehry has described to me as a refusal to play.

In wanting, then, with the architect's help, to describe his work first and foremost in terms of its architectural programme, I have thought it important to try to get to its poetics without losing sight of its affirmative practicality. His buildings are critically informed but motivated by a wish to create an activity rather than to react, and exist to be used as well as seen. Events rather than speculations, they may be sculptural but are not sculpture. I begin, therefore, with an early public building that illustrates the practicality of Gehry's approach while setting the stage, or site, for his poetics.

The Concord Performing Arts Pavilion (1974–77; fig 1) in Concord, California, may seem like an odd (even improbable) place to begin a discussion of Gehry's work. In some respects atypical, it is unlikely to be the building one thinks of first when Gehry's name is mentioned. But it is a good representative of his approach: it preserves what is inherently valuable in the site while responding to its physical and social exigencies, without surrendering any of the programme's intrinsic possibilities to the task of making such a response. Gehry's use of continuity and discontinuity provides a clue to how he does this. It crops up everywhere in his work as a principle through which the building may, in part, be thought of as a structure of complementary but also contradictory and even mutually exclusive movements.

The site plan for the Pavilion indicates that the wind blows traffic noise onto the site. Both come from the north west, the one amplifying the other by carrying it towards the building—nature and culture collaborating to intensify one another as negative functions. Their notation locates the building within the auditory aspect of its context, taking the plan beyond describing the relationship of a form to a topography to become instead a description of the circumstances in which the building acts. The traffic noise is an invisible but determining factor in the programme's realisation.

Fig. 1 Frank Gehry & Associates: Concord Pavillion, Concord, Californian, 1974–1977 (renovated 1994–1996). Photo: Morley Baer, 1977

Gehry has also said of the Concord Pavilion that he liked the foothills that lie behind it and didn't want the building to get in their way. The opposite of the tower or steeple on a hill that becomes both armature and frame for a spectacle, rendering the scene picturesque by making nature coalesce around and in relation to it, the Concord Pavilion nestles into a hollow and invites the viewer to look at the hills as well as at the building, and not necessarily at the same time—ie, not necessarily in terms of one another. The building, then, takes into account the fact that the site is prone to wind and traffic noise, and is in part a product of a desire to leave the landscape alone as far as possible. This regard for both the social programme and the landscape's beauty did not, however, lead Gehry to try to make a building that is in any way self-effacing—if such a description could ever be appropriate to a large structure placed in the middle of an open space. The Concord Pavilion may stay out of the way of both the wind and the view, but in arranging for it to do so, Gehry makes a distinction between fitting in and blending in.

Anything produced by late twentieth-century technology and placed in the California desert is likely to look like something out of a science-fiction movie—the contrast between an expansive landscape bathed in the clarity of the desert and the impeccable forms of the machine-made guarantees it. And it is where the science-fiction films of the 1950s and 1960s were made, ensuring California's control of the look of the future. If you see an image of the future set in a desert, it is quite likely that you're really looking at a picture of California. Significantly, the same will be true if you're looking at an image of the national frontier myth set in the past. Apart from its location, the Concord Pavilion further encourages the analogy with science fiction by being saucer-like, or possibly Stealth Bomber-like, seeming at once set in place and disassociated from its surroundings, detachable from them, self-sufficient, alien, possibly ready to take off at any time. One might say that it is detached from its natural surroundings by not being *of* them—not built out of local materials, not coloured to match the landscape—but at the same time attached to them at the level of the iconic, in that both the building and the landscape have associations with science fiction and thus with one another. Here, however, one should note that it really is a technologically active building. As a top-of-the-line example of the latest in flexible performance spaces it is full of electrically driven moving parts. It is not an image of the future like a vehicle in a film set in a time yet to come that is actually propelled by the technology of today. It is today's latest, a thing produced by, as well as a sign of, a present (already a past therefore, a historical object and object of history) defined by a certain technological capacity. In this, it deploys the iconography of the futuristic in the interests of the present rather than the reverse. However atypical its appearance may be, then, its preoccupation with the contemporary is typical Gehry.

The extent to which not blending in is a function of the Concord Pavilion's materials and design may be seen by comparing it with Gehry's Merriweather Post Pavilion of Music in Baltimore (1967), a shed that shares with its Arcadian surroundings a thoroughly low- (or as far as possible no-) tech attitude to life. As a response to the programme and its context, the Concord Pavilion fits into the landscape by allowing for the wind and traffic noise and by preserving the continuity of the horizon. But it does not blend into it visually as the Merriweather building does, presenting itself instead as an alien object that defamiliarises (has an alienating effect on) its natural and naturalised surroundings. Interrupting as little as possible of that which it must inevitably alter, the Concord Pavilion in effect uses its surroundings to articulate its own difference from them through a continuity grounded in that difference. As a gesture that keeps the landscape intact, it remains outside it, but joined to it by the gesture.

Difference and continuity in Gehry's work are functions of how materials signify in it. His work makes itself felt as an organisation of materials that may dissolve into visual effects while simultaneously retaining their original identity, but this is not a dissolving or subsuming of materiality into an array of references to an instituted (largely by those making the references) architectural discourse—and even less a question of reorienting the latter to a language of representation. If others have turned architecture into a semiotics of one sort or another—of popular conventions in the case of Robert Venturi, of the intellectually esoteric in that of Eisenman for example—Gehry's work invokes a sense of architecture as a hermeneutics as much as any structuralism of connotation and recognition.

If only because his is an architectural practice as, or more, concerned with what is present than what is represented, the question of Gehry's use of materials leads to one that asks how the building is where it is, how it reinvents location through dislocation. Many other things about Gehry's architecture could lead to the phenomenology of Maurice Merleau-Ponty, to how things touch, to the subject's realisation of the world as a totality of the seen and the unseen, where the latter strains towards expression in the visible. But Gehry's use of materials and site leads to Heidegger, because the latter explained most persuasively that how anything got to where it is, figures into its being what it is.

Gehry flourishes in a world that Heidegger foresaw, in some respects quite accurately, with loathing. But despite this difference between them, comparison with Heidegger's hermeneutics follows naturally or logically from Gehry's attitude to the site and what to put there. It seems to come down to the preservation of different kinds of discontinuity between the site and the building. Or to discontinuities that serve different needs, and even those differences threaten to dissolve or collapse into each other as one approaches the final analysis. (But while finalities of whatever variety do always seem to have a lot in common, this can be misleading.) Discontinuity in Heidegger preserves through transforming by making the process of transformation itself a realisation of the signifying potential of what is to be preserved—the temple made out of local stone, place rendered into form. When Gehry wants to preserve something, for example the view of the foothills behind the Concord Pavilion, he leaves it alone and does something in response to it that may follow from it but that can also come from somewhere else.

With regard to the physical context, Gehry's buildings range from interventions in the landscape that respond to it but have no apparent material or other continuity with it, save at the very important level of proposing a thematic or atmospheric association of one sort or another, as in the Concord Pavilion, to interventions in cityscapes that respond both to the local materials and to the general visual and social configuration of the milieu, of which the American Center in Paris (1994; figs 2, 3) is an example. (One may say then that human order, building and the social, at first sight at least, call for a more overt response from Gehry than does God's order—unlike foothills, the human requires reorientation if not reordering.) Whether there are other buildings around or not, Gehry's work does something that seems in one sense consistent, and in another inconsistent, with Heidegger's example of a Greek temple as a reformulation of the landscape into a sign,

Fig. 2 (top) Frank Gehry & Associates: American Center, Paris, 1988–1994. Photo: Erich Ansel Koyama 1974

Fig. 3 (left) Frank Gehry & Associates: American Center, Paris, 1988–1994. Photo: Erich Ansel Koyama 1974

earth into world, in *The Origin of the Work of Art*.[4] The point being that it is in Heidegger's approach to the same question, that of discontinuity and continuity between the building and its context, that both consistency and inconsistency may be found.

Heidegger's temple is made out of the rock on which it stands. Gehry's building is nothing of the sort. Heidegger's building is there as a reformulation of the already present, while Gehry's adds to it. Gehry's work is not, like certain strands of Modernism grounded in functionalism, programmatically indifferent to the Heideggerian problematic. It invites comparison with it because it can seem to come close to it. But contemporary culture places a high value on placelessness, standing Heidegger on his head, and it is because of Gehry's very different attitude to how to relate to the site that his practice flourishes in—rather than being destroyed by—a world that Heidegger regarded as nightmarish. Gehry sees it as needing considerable improvement.

Karsten Harries, while taking note of the impracticality of a discussion predicated on a wholesale rejection of technology, and also of the potentially debilitating effect of Heidegger's predilection for the hyperbolic, puts the claims Heidegger makes for architecture succinctly:

> As a seemingly self-sufficient presence the temple draws our attention, putting its setting at a distance. Thus distanced, the setting is, so to speak, put in a frame. Framed, it is represented. The temple thus lets us look again not just at itself, at its form and materials, but at its site. By confronting its context instead of quietly submitting to it, the work of architecture becomes a light that illuminates its surroundings, including other buildings.[5]

To paraphrase Louis Namier's famous remark about religion being the name by which politics was known in the seventeenth century, within the modern and its consequences 'alienates' refers to what used to be meant by 'illuminates'.

If the Concord Pavilion frames unobtrusively, in effect framing by not obscuring or interrupting, Gehry's proposed revision of Berlin's Museum Island would have been an elaborate reframing, while everyone seems to agree that the Guggenheim Museum in Bilbao may be described as a confirmation of Heidegger's image of a light that illuminates what surrounds it. In Gehry's urban projects especially, the history of the site is folded into its elaborate reconsideration as more than a historical index, what surrounds the building being more than a summary of its past.

Before returning to Gehry's relationship to his time, or his buildings' relationship to the contexts in which they occur, I want first to say something about their 'self-sufficiency', to use Harries' word for it. In Heidegger's description, the site literally provides the raw materials for the idea, in part developed out of it, through which it is to be transformed. In Gehry's work the materials come from elsewhere, and are industrial rather than raw. The self-sufficiency of one of his buildings is in this respect double-edged: it may look as if it came from elsewhere, but it is through this apparently arbitrary relationship to the site, underscored by its discontinuity with it as a material assemblage, that it reframes its context in a way soon seen to be anything but arbitrary.

Over the years, Gehry's buildings have become curvy, their self-sufficiency underscored by the intrinsic relationships of complex forms that are not mirrored in those that surround them as verticals and horizontals would be. (How they rediscover what surrounds them is a large part of the content of the Museum Island proposal, discussed in Chapter 2.) While having many ramifications, this curviness may be related to Gehry's treatment of what one would suppose to be a fundamental aspect of architectural self-sufficiency—the relationship of the roof to the rest. If one compares the Concord Pavilion to the much later Experience Music Project (Seattle, begun 1998; figs 4, 5), one moves from straight lines to no straight lines at all, and from a very clear set of oppositions between vertical and horizontal to a grouping of forms in which the distinction between roof and wall has been obviated, or blurred, or otherwise suspended or deferred.

Fig. 4 Frank Gehry & Associates: Experience Music Project, Seattle, 1995–2000, design process model. Photo: Joshua White, 1997 © FOG&A

Fig. 5 Frank Gehry & Associates: Experience Music Project, Seattle, 1995–2000, design process model. Photo: Joshua White, 1997 © FOG&A

The Experience Music Project exhibits a body-like mobility (whose implications will be further pursued here in discussing the Disney Concert Hall), which is characteristic of Gehry's later work, where curves sometimes define forms and at others belong to surfaces or planes that are clearly free to move with some independence of the forms they cover and inflect. Curvature, in Gehry's work of the past decade or more, allows the building to bulge and flow, constantly folding in on itself, offering continuous surfaces where one expects a disjunction between wall and roof, front and side, leaving room for different kinds of disjunctions, between curves that do not follow from others except as counter-movements, movements summoned up in order to act against, or in some other kind of complementary opposition to, others, to which they may relate by having little in common but the question of relationship. The Concord Pavilion is exciting because it is all roof, open to what it frames by not obliterating, a platform from which music leaks into the desert. But the Experience Music Project is also, albeit in quite another way, all roof. Spreading out horizontally—like the Concord building—it is a little bit like a landscape, replete with sharp and shallow inclines, a gentle valley and a deep canyon.

The model of the Experience Music Project reproduced, and discussed, here (which is not the version that was actually built—an example of Gehry accommodating the client, who found it too extreme), also demonstrates the potential for colour in Gehry's departure from the strictly rectilinear. The continuous skin of this building may be related to the fish, whose form is at once streamlined and made of an articulated surface, and which has been a major source of inspiration for Gehry. It may also be related to sculpture—in sculptures the top may be the same as the sides, which is not customarily the case in a building, where the roof is normally expected to be different from the walls that support it. The use of colour put forward here, however, derives from, and points to, neither.

The model uses two kinds of colour: the metallic colour of the building's cladding, and the colour that has been added on—red and white. (Later, purple would be brought into play.) Only one form in the model is unified by—is allowed to be—a single colour, and that is the white closed wing at the right that balances in its completeness the openness of the other end. This balance is confirmed in the relationship between the crumpled covering of the right-hand, white wall and the layered, multi-directional drama of openness taking place at the building's other extreme.

Elsewhere, the building uses colour to complicate continuity, to interrupt it in ways that have no immediately apparent relationship to the surfaces that are interrupted, and to add to it a further possibility for something like weightlessness. The red in this model has antecedents throughout art history from Pompeian painting to Matisse's *Red Studio*, and does in all of them what it does here: in threatening to detach itself from the surface it covers, to float off and away from it, it intensifies the form that surface describes by offering to dissolve it. Red is too intense not to act against the form that supports it, which is here either gold, conventionally the colour of light and therefore weightlessness, or white, lightness incarnate. These three conditions of the anti-gravitational are encountered in this model along, and as, the side of a large building that is made of curves. In other places one finds silver and gold—giving way to red and white on two sides—in an interaction that responds to the big differences in shape as the intersecting of movements that take place across the top of the building, spilling over onto the sides to create an effect almost of a building designed from the top, but according to a principle that leads from there directly to the ground, without an intervening break between roof and wall. Where the Concord Pavilion almost disappears into the hollow prepared for it, re-emerging in absolute rectilinear and horizontal opposition to the undulating verticality of the mountains behind it, the Experience Music Project shifts within itself in terms of volumes rather than planes. Alternating between generally vertical movements and ones that are correspondingly generally horizontal, with Gehry constantly finding ways—particularly on the roof—to stir up or fray out surfaces where they intersect, the Experience Music Project leaves the ground and returns to it as digressively as forms weave around one another within the scheme as a whole. Colour is used to add complexity to the already complex, but also—as with the shape the red makes on the roof—to focus and identify while at the same time making the point focused upon a transition to elsewhere—in this case, the red comes to point in four different directions. It seems central to the complication of the complicated—a theme of this use of colour—that red is used to introduce shapes into the building that would otherwise not be there. The red describes a form complete where it covers and follows a corner, but open at its other sides in a distant echo of the building's theme of self-enclosure on the one side and opening-out on the other.

With Gehry, one gets to the main course right away. That's why I like his architecture. I find in it what I find in Pollock, or Beethoven, where everything is also all there from the first sight or sound. There's no preparatory phase that gets you ready for something more elaborate, it's already very elaborate. One's attention is held from the start by the complexity of the experience, including elements of which one may not be consciously aware until a little time has passed.

The syntax and effect of Gehry's buildings have changed since the Concord Pavilion was built, their immediacy of a different order now from then, but the approach to the programme has not altered all that much. For example, the Disney Concert Hall proceeds from a cube, as do many of his earlier buildings, and in its simplicity, the Concord Pavilion is a bit like the programme that excited Heidegger: geometry reformulating geology through scale derived from the human rather than the landscape. To extend the comparison of differences and similarities, in the Concord Pavilion, work as design is the same thing as in Heidegger's version, and work as engineering is not. Crucially, the building does not seek to conquer or overwhelm the landscape into which it is inserted, but to have an interaction with it that is based in large part on difference—not only the ideas that construct it but the materials used in it come from elsewhere— and relationships of non-relationship. If, then, its placement and design unite it with the landscape in another manner and for some other reason than that proposed by Heidegger, at least the immediately apprehensible clarity of the Concord Pavilion is not difficult to reconcile with the minimal presentationalism that Heidegger sees in the Greek temple. This is especially true with respect to the straight-forwardness of its opposition, as the basis of reintegration, of human scale and human work to the sublime extensiveness of unpopulated landscape.

However, if the Concord Pavilion sets itself forth, to use Heidegger's language, through a lateral rectilinearity—its use of horizontality being what unites it with the landscape, and the absence of undulation what sets it apart—by the time one reaches the Experience Music Project, not only has the idea of landscape become a possibility within the building itself— undulation being inherent in curves where it is not in straight lines—but the architectural programme is presented quite differently and has become something quite different.

One may see the later works as elaborations, remorseless pursuits of a basic logic, taken in new directions by, inter alia, new materials. But that is by no means an adequate account of what one sees. Where the Concord Pavilion makes use of diagonals to integrate its programme with its context, images of speed suspended—fast lateral movement on stilts, a roof angled out towards infinity—the Experience Music Project is multi-directional, explicitly complicated where the earlier building is minimal, made of many movements instead of a few. It is an architecture of trajectories as much as forms, in which a plurality of movements converge as much in mutual distraction as consolidation, designed for subjectivities as mobile and decentred as itself. Yet Gehry's highly concentrated architecture allows for moments of relaxation, as in those aspects of his buildings that one can only describe in negative terms, like 'unfussy'. This may be read as a rejection of fussiness but, rather than a critical gesture, it reflects a fascination with approximation as a visual effect.

To Heidegger, capitalism in its later form was a nightmare. This was because he felt that technology had abolished time, and with it a sense of space as lived as opposed to traversed.[6] In substituting a world pictured—which is to say, rendered simultaneous—for a world experienced as presence and presence as absence, technology undermines man's ability to have a relationship with it on any but a utilitarian plane.[7] Everything is presented at man's disposal and from his point of view, but for that very reason this becomes the only way he can relate to it. Nor is that all. For Heidegger, the technological abolition of distance is the abolition of difference and with it the continuity of space with time: 'All distances in time and space are shrinking ... The peak of this abolition of every possibility of remoteness is reached by television, which will soon pervade and dominate the whole machinery of communication'.[8] The farmer once knew his neighbour and experienced neighbourliness as a function of the distance between the two farms, separate but contiguous, temporally apart while set together in space, whereas 'Today everything present is equally near and equally far. But no abridging or abolishing of distances brings nearness'.[9] The telephone, for example, literally robs distance of significance, disembodying the idea of proximity and replacing it with electronic immediacy. To Heidegger this distracts from one's sense of one's mortality, without which one cannot be human—an awareness of the inevitability of death being what underlies and structures consciousness of life as temporally as well as spatially finite. His position on the question regarding technology could also be related to the reluctance with which the authorities accepted Galileo's telescope (which we know wasn't actually his) because it contradicted Aristotle and the use to which mediaeval and Jesuitical theology had put his thinking. The telescope demonstrated that an instrument could be superior to the naked eye—there are mountains on the moon but it looks smooth to unassisted vision—while Aristotle had been interpreted as insisting that human perception was always the final arbiter of apparent truth.

If Gehry thrives in the world pictured by a techno-capitalism whose post-war emergence distressed Heidegger—who identified it with America—perhaps that is because he has been able to think practically, not being fundamentally unsympathetic to the difficulty posed by a world of the placeless, of the deoriginated. There may be something to the thought that living in Los Angeles—rather than, say, New York—has provided him with a certain insight into it. To a very large degree, Los Angeles embodies Heidegger's nightmare. That includes the things that make it a pleasant place in which to live. It is a piece of desert that has been made to conform as far as possible to the appearance of the temperate, held together by automobiles washed regularly with water brought from hundreds of miles away. If more or less every living thing in Europe came, prehistorically, from Anatolia, as seems to have been the case, that was something Heidegger seemed able to forget, but Los Angeles is a heterogeneity of people who came from elsewhere within living, or thoroughly recorded, memory.

At the same time, it is at the centre of much of everything in the world. As noted, everybody has seen it before they arrive. To live in it is, perhaps, to have the world picture as a condition of everyday life: it is the home of the other through which the world sees itself—the screen image—as well as being literally a place developed through displacement—the temperate into the desert, culturally as well as ecologically. As a condition of everyday life, in which one begins with the unrooted, the—homeless—as the German so tellingly has it, it is the origin of much of the world that the world sees at home. It is in this sense that one feels Gehry's architecture has been conditioned by Los Angeles in very straightforward ways—especially by the earthquake codes—but also in ways that have excited less comment. This would suggest that one should approach Gehry's work not only through its material or iconic associations with Los Angeles, but also through the idea of the human subject that has emerged within it, or been constructed by it, over the years. This would be a subject that lived in and through the deoriginated and the mobile, ie, one more obviously or thoroughly developed in Los Angeles, the capital city of suburbs, than in the older, centred cities of America's East Coast.

Perhaps the realisation of such a subject—one able, for example, to think of movement as the status quo rather than a departure from it—requires something other than continuity of the sort provided by Heidegger's temple. Were the Concord Pavilion to have been made out of stone cut from the mountains behind it, it would not only have fallen down in an earthquake, but would also have looked absurd because it owes so much to its resemblance to a spaceship. It fits into its landscape by not being of it, and Concord is not even in Los Angeles County, but further north, where people believe that Los Angeles treats nature with the contempt that it shows for the idea of origin. The two areas are linked, however, by a state ideology that precludes stone not only because insurance companies eschew fatalism, but also because of its faith in the impermanent as a value. Even were it practical to do so, which it is not thanks to the tendency towards violent mobility of the local geology, it would not be appropriate to build anything in Los Angeles out of the local stone. But, as an option, you can clad a building with anything, including stone. It just cannot support anything. If it tries to it falls down. Early versions of the Disney Concert Hall were clad in stone, associating that material with movement (a property foreign to it), while depriving it of a structural function.

Baudrillard has suggested that Utah exists to prove the existence of God, California to prove the existence of happiness (two devotions to that which may not be intellectually verified).[10] Mormons build stone monstrosities that are indeed temples, but the state of happiness is one of automobility and moving images; redemption (ie pleasure) in the freedom to move, and the image that changes, is made not of stone but light, California's icon of permanence. When southern California turns to God, it builds the Crystal Cathedral, the Perpendicular Style blended with Kew Gardens in a monumental, if banal, fusion of the spirituality of light with technology.[11] This may be a Walt Disney version of the mediaeval, providing God with the opportunity to come up with lighting effects at least comparable to those the congregation is used to seeing in Las Vegas, but in that respect it is significantly unlike the Mormon preference for something that looks vaguely like an Assyrian mausoleum. The God that lives in the Crystal Cathedral believes in capitalism but otherwise preaches tolerance (of all but poverty) while the Mormon God will kill you if you even think of fucking around. The culture of southern California would have difficulty with buildings made of stone even if there weren't earthquakes because it places no inherent value on either fixity or authentic origin, and for that reason the petrified and weighty have restricted appeal, while remaining tremendously popular in zones that continue to be driven by ancestor worship and infatuation with the ascetic.[12]

Accordingly, Gehry used stone in the early versions of the Disney Concert Hall but made it behave as an image of its opposite: mobile, anti-gravitational, supporting nothing and the foundation of nothing. But when in ancestor-worshipping zones, he is more likely to incorporate stone cladding into the building as a sign of permanence—that is to say, still as sign rather than support, certainly, but one that signifies in the traditional way—which should give pause to those who accuse him of seeking to turn Europe into an imitation California. Unlike the pre-metallic versions of the Disney Concert Hall, his European projects do not turn stone against itself, although— especially in the Bilbao Guggenheim—they use glass and reflection to lift it up. Stone is not a counterweight to the lightness of other materials in Gehry's European projects so much as it is continuous with them as a minimum degree of the weightlessness of which they become maxima. In the American Centre in Paris he used 'the kind of stone that all of Paris was made of' and in the Bilbao Guggenheim 'the same stone they have [t]here. It's from a small quarry in Granada. They almost didn't have enough. We pushed them right to the edge of what they had'.13

Gehry's combination of the local stone with an entirely new building material, titanium, in the Bilbao Guggenheim, is fundamental to the building's meaning. *Der Spiegel*'s characterisation of his architecture as a practice in which 'if you look closer at Gehry's buildings, the original nimbus disappears. Its typical style is spread all over Europe',14 is simply wrong, but it could be usefully rephrased. If one looks more closely at the buildings mentioned by *Der Spiegel*—the Bilbao Guggenheim, the American Center in Paris, the Vitra Furniture Museum in Weil am Rhein (1987) and the Nationale-Nederlanden building in Prague (1996), one sees that what they have in common is what links them, without eroding their individuality, to the world as it is now.

Notes

1. Peter Arnell and Ted Bickford (eds), *Frank Gehry: Buildings and Projects*, Rizzoli, New York, 1985, pp xiv–xv.
2. Kurt W Forster, in a taped conversation with the author, 5 September 1988.
3. Scott Gutterman, 'Frankly Speaking', *Guggenheim Magazine*, XI, Fall 1997, p 26.
4. Martin Heidegger, 'the Origin of the Work of Art', in *Poetry, Language, Thought*, trans Albert Hofstadter, Harper & Row, New York, 1971.
5. Karsten Harries, *The Ethical Function of Architecture*, MIT Press, Cambridge, Mass, 1997, pp 279–280.
6. 'The fundamental event of the modern age is the conquest of the world as picture. The word 'picture' [*Bild*], now means the structured image [*Gebild*] that is the creature of man's producing which represents and sets before'. Heidegger, 'The Age of the World Picture', in *The Question Concerning Technology*, trans and intro William Lovett, Harper & Rowe, New York, 1977, p 134.
7. 'The hydroelectric plant is not built into the Rhine river as was the old wooden bridge which joined bank to bank for hundreds of years... What the river is now, namely, a water power supplier, derives from out of the essence of the power stations. In order that we may even remotely consider the monstrousness of what reigns here, let us ponder the contrast that speaks out of the two titles, 'The Rhine' as damned up into the *power* works, and 'The Rhine' as uttered out of the *art* work, in Holderlin's hymn of that name. But, it will be replied, the Rhine is still a river in a landscape, is it not? Perhaps. But how? In no other way

than as an object on call for inspection by a tour group ordered there by the vacation industry'. Heidegger, 'The Question Concerning Technology', op cit, p 16.

8. Heidegger, 'The Thing', in *Poetry, Language, Thought*, op cit, p 165.

9. Heidegger, op cit, p 177.

10. 'The Californians are committed to a job of advertising just as ascetic as the task of the Mormons with whom they share a geographical and mental space. They are a huge sect devoted to proving happiness, as others have dedicated themselves to the greater glory of God.' Jean Baudrillard, *Cool Memories II*, trans Chris Turner, Polity Press, Cambridge, 1996, p 41.

11. Paralleling, in this but nothing else, what Harries has to say about Gropius and the Bauhaus: 'Projecting [an] idealised past into the future Gropius dreams of an architecture that once again will be "the crystalline expression of man's noblest thought, his ardour, his humanity, his faith, his religion!" But "faith" here means faith in reason and in the solidarity of liberated humanity. The new cathedral envisioned by Gropius is very much a socialist cathedral. And it is a cathedral to be built on the basis of technology'. Harries, op cit, pp 330–31.

12. Harries, who seems to like ancestor worship but not asceticism, turns to Nietzsche on the stone question: '[Nietzsche's] statement about the masklike beauty of modern architecture occurs in the section of *Human, All Too Human* entitled "Stone is more stone than it used to be". Stone used to be more than just stone; it also had a meaning. Stone spoke and helped architecture to speak. As postmodern architecture rediscovered, buildings once had something of the quality of texts, as did nature. Today we stand before both without understanding'. (Harries, op cit, p 347.)

Whether or not the last two sentences contradict one another—one soon realises that Harries is paraphrasing Nietzsche, but somehow postmodernism has been interposed between sentences—it is to the point that Nietzsche saw that industrialism had sucked the expressive primacy out of the landscape's most fundamental material, but that his position (too) is surprisingly humanistic from a contemporary perspective (Apollonian or even Christian in its unusual hostility to beauty). It is worth quoting him more completely: 'We have outgrown the symbolism of lines and figures, as we have grown unaccustomed to the tonal effect of rhetoric, no longer having sucked in this kind of cultural mother's milk from the first moment of life. Originally, everything about a Greek or Christian building meant something... in reference to a higher order of things. This atmosphere of inexhaustible meaningfulness hung about the building like a magic veil. Beauty entered the system only secondarily, impairing the basic feeling of uncanny sublimity, of sanctification by magic or the gods' nearness. At the most, beauty tempered the dread—but this dread was a prerequisite everywhere. What does the beauty of a building mean to us now? The same as the beautiful face of a mindless woman: something masklike', (Frederick Nietzsche, *Human, All Too Human*, intro Marion Faber, trans M. Faber with Stephen Lehmann, University of Nebraska Press, Lincoln, Nebraska, 1984, p 131.

The contemporary has indeed outgrown that past, but growing could in this sense be thought of as something that happens whether one wants it to or not (as Harries knows well, see op cit p 254), and one might ask what kind of Peter Panism is it that wants to associate beauty and the masklike with mindlessness? (For the elements of an alternative view, see my 'Blankness as a Signifier', *Critical Inquiry*, XXIV, 1, Autumn 1997).

13.	Gutterman, op cit, p 26.
14.	'Sonnen-Pop im Nebelland' ('Sun Pop in the Hazyland'), *Der Speigel*, XXXVIII, 1994, pp 200–203.

CHAPTER 2
Berlin: The Preservation of Insulation

Why does one set of ideas have to kill another set? I really believe that there should be more than one system, because if you have more than one system, then no one single system prevails.

Less insular than its name implies, Berlin's Museum Island is in fact only the northern tip of an island, its site beginning where a canal separates from the River Spree, but bounded at the south by the Unter den Linden. It is occupied by five museums, built at different times, disconnected and approached from various directions. The southernmost museum is the Altes, built by Karl Friedrick Schinkel between 1823 and 1830. The Altes Museum faces and is entered from the Unter den Linden by way of the Lustgarten—the latter at the time of writing undergoing reinvention along postmodernist lines by the sculptor Gerhard Merz in collaboration with the architect OM Ungers. The Altes is separated from the Alte Nationalgalerie and the Pergamon and Neues Museums by Bodestrasse, across which it is joined to the latter by a long-disused, covered footbridge. The Bode is at the northernmost end of the site, separated from the others by an elevated railway bridge, which carries the S-Bahn over the canal and the river. Dietrich Wildung, of the Agyptiches Museum und Paypyrussamlung (part of the Pergamon), has perhaps given the most succinct description of what is worthwhile about Gehry's proposal for the Museum Island's restoration and redevelopment:

> Over and above its optimal functionality, Frank Gehry's design has a surprising effect, especially with regard to the aspects of monument preservation and city planning. Through the new buildings on the Kupfergraben, he turns the historic buildings into objects of critical reflection without taking away their dignity, thus actualising the building history of the Museum Island and leading it to a spectacular goal.[1]

Wildung begins by acknowledging Gehry's practicality—the 'optimal functionality' of his proposal—and then goes on to couple its effect of surprise with aspects of planning and preservation. In his second sentence he repeats the idea in detail: Gehry has achieved a critical reflection that preserves the dignity of the historical buildings, permitting their pasts to be actualised in a way that culminates in a spectacle that intensifies what is already there. The crucial terms in this sentence are 'historic', 'critical', 'dignity', and 'spectacular'. The historical is subjected to criticism—of a sort where the object and the grounds of the critical are the historical—but the spectacle that results is made out of what that criticism preserves rather than being something that fills a void left by what critical reflection may have taken away.

Gehry was initially reluctant to enter the competition for the Museum Island project, the first round of which was held in 1994. This was because he could see that if he won, he'd have to be in Berlin regularly and 'the thought of going to Berlin once a month for the rest of my life didn't seem appropriate'. Describing the site as 'a holy place', he saw that this would be a project fraught with the difficulties that accompany the sacred, namely, arguments about interpretation. He was persuaded to enter by Wolf Dube, Director of Berlin's Museums, with whom he had worked in 1992 when he designed the installation for Stefanie Barron's reconstitution of Hitler's 'Degenerate Art' exhibition, which originated at the Los Angeles County Museum of Art and subsequently moved to the Altes. Dube would like to see the Museum Island become a major tourist attraction, comparable to the Louvre. Mention of the Louvre causes his detractors to aver that under no circumstances must the Museum Island become a shopping mall. What this has turned out to mean is that, as far as possible, the revision of the site must contain no new ideas about architecture.

Gehry's involvement with the project had three stages. The first, the master plan for the whole complex, is what will be discussed here (1994, figs 6–12, 18, 19). The second replaced curvature with rectilinearity and attempted to provide a less exciting but more restrained version of his original plan for a bridge linking the Neues Museum with the Altes (1997, fig 13). That stage and the third (also 1997, fig 14), largely restricted to an interior design for the Neues, whose exterior (fig 15) was now to be preserved rehabilitated but unconcealed, are monuments to Gehry's persistence in trying to address the programme while pleasing a client who has become possessed of an uninteresting idea. The revised bridge was a compromise with the aesthetic that the jury had by then shown itself to favour, while the rejection of his interior design for the Neues (figs 16, 17) goes to the heart of the difficulty he had with the project almost from the start. He was working with a client who wanted to preserve everything because it was sacred.

That Gehry's proposal was not accepted might, then, have been the result of either incomprehension—the jury didn't understand the critical reflection—or the opposite: they understood it all right, they just didn't like it. As Wildung makes clear, however, the people who work there did like it and still do. The following brief narrative of the project's development to date suggests that insensitivity to the needs of the Museum Island as a group of museums, as opposed to a national shrine, has not been helpful.

The City of Berlin decided to rehabilitate the Museum Island, which had not flourished under late Stalinism, in the euphoria that followed reunification. City planners and other government officials chose the jury for the competition for the master plan, which was accordingly weighted so as

Fig. 6 Frank Gehry & Associates: Museum Island, Berlin, competition model, Phase One,
Photo: Joshua White, 1994 © FOG&A

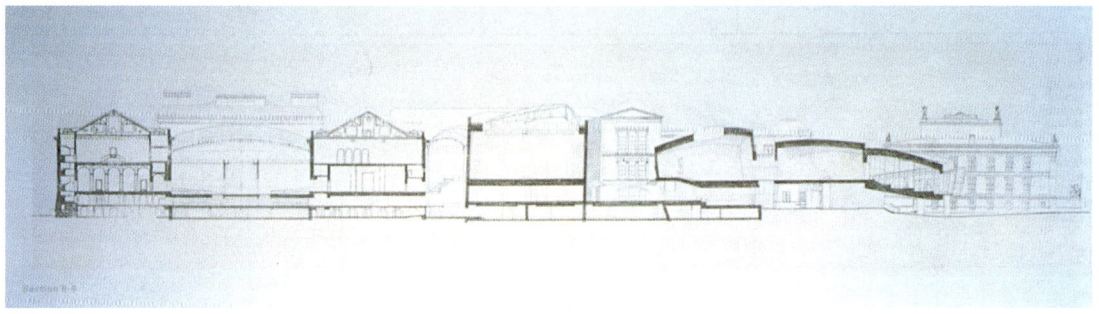

Fig. 7 Frank Gehry & Associates: Museum Island, Berlin, competition model (drawing). Phase
One Photo: Joshua White, 1994 © FOG&A

not to give decisive power to the museums' representatives. As remarked,
Dube's ambitions for Museum Island were regarded with suspicion by those
who wished, above all, to be reassured that the complex would survive as a
sign of the seriousness with which official Berlin takes the idea of culture.
Some would also say that the jury was weighted in favour of the
architectural tendency known as The New Minimalism—which was
extremely fashionable at that moment—and perhaps that tendency's innate
bias against innovation led to the selection of a candidate, Giorgio Grassi, a
New Minimalist who seemed to represent a compromise between great

Fig. 8 Frank Gehry & Associates: Museum Island, Berlin, competition model, Phase One, Photo: Joshua White, 1994 © FOG&A

Fig. 9 Frank Gehry & Associates: Museum Island, Berlin, competition model, Phase One, Photo: Joshua White, 1994 © FOG&A

34   *Berlin: The Preservation of Insulation*

Fig. 10 Frank Gehry & Associates: Museum Island, Berlin, competition model, Phase One, Photo: Joshua White, 1994 © FOG&A

Fig. 11 Frank Gehry & Associates: Museum Island, Berlin, competition model, Phase One, Photo: Joshua White, 1994 © FOG&A

Fig. 12 Frank Gehry & Associates: Museum Island, Berlin, competition model, Phase One, Photo: Joshua White, 1994 © FOG&A

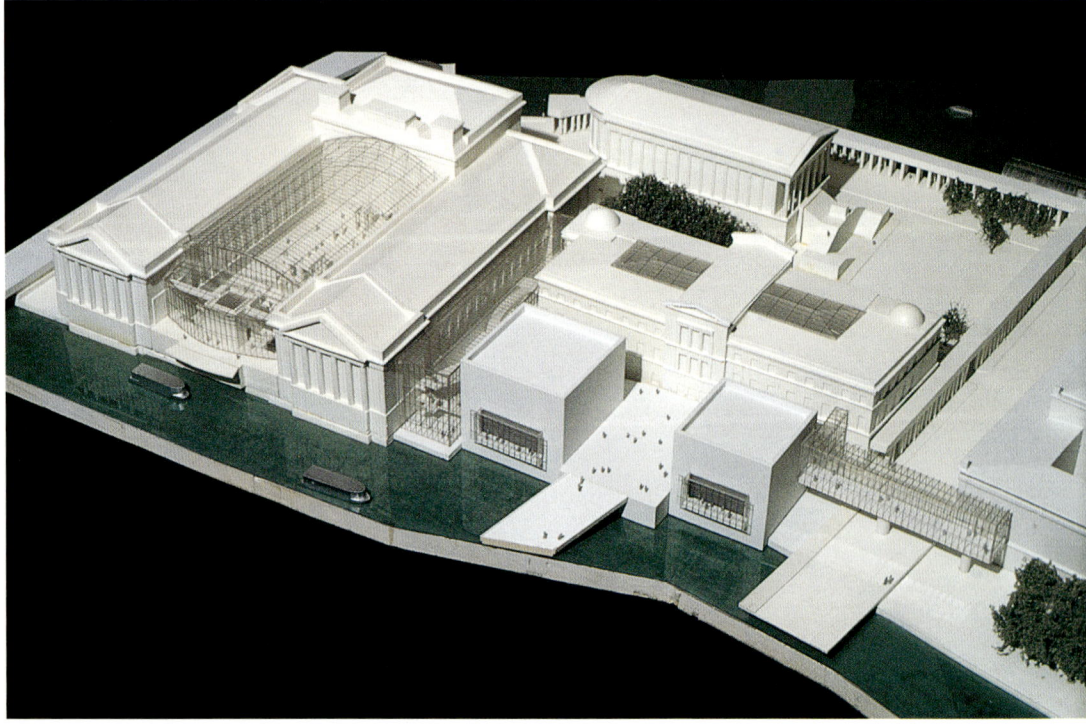

Fig. 13 Frank Gehry & Associates: Museum Island, Berlin, competition model, Phase Two, Photo: Joshua White, 1997 © FOG&A

Fig. 14 Frank Gehry & Associates: Museum island, Berlin, competition model, Phase Two, Photo: Joshua White, 1997 © FOG&A

Fig. 15 Frederich Stüler: Neues Museum, 1843–1859, Museum Island, Berlin, Germany

Fig. 16 Frank Gehry & Associates: Museum Island, Berlin, competition model, Phase Three, Photo: Joshua White, 1997 © FOG&A

Fig. 17 Frank Gehry & Associates: Museum Island, Berlin, competition model, Phase Three, Photo: Joshua White, 1997 © FOG&A

change and none. He was perceived as neither extreme and mad, like Gehry, nor as a simple, or preposterous, conservative. But the compromise failed: Grassi withdrew from the project after eighteen months because he could not persuade the museums' curatorial staffs to agree to his programme.

The jury then turned to David Chippendale, the runner-up—also a New Minimalist. By this time, the project had dwindled—following changes in government policy dictated by the sudden lack of money produced by reunification—to a more limited reformation of the site, focused on, and more or less restricted to, the Neues. At the time of writing, the curators fail to see how they can work with Chippendale's programme either. Gehry's proposal showed that he had worked with the curators in mind, and with the administrative programme's call for easy access to all the museums for tourists and other visitors. He has designed many exhibitions and knows what curators do. The committee freaked out because of what Gehry's proposal looked like, while the curators have fought to adopt as much of his programme as possible in the face of those elements that the jury's decisions have imposed upon them. Gehry came fourth in the competition for the master plan, and has been in and out of it again since Grassi's withdrawal. One may say that four differences of opinion, judgement, or belief, poisoned his relationship to the project. Firstly, his attitude to the site and what it means to Berlin was at best misunderstood and at worst misrepresented. Secondly, his idea that the museum complex is something that could be improved rather than uncritically preserved didn't help. Thirdly, and more specifically, his sense of the Neues as a weak element that required much reform amounted to a final heresy. Fourthly, the gap between Gehry's thinking—inflected as it is by the old Minimalism—and New Minimalism made things difficult from the beginning, given the majority of the jury's predisposition to an architectural style that is all that his is not.

Taking the fourth point last, while it is not the purpose of this discussion to criticise either Grassi or Chippendale—the concern here being exclusively with the implications of Gehry's proposal for an understanding of his ideas about architecture—it is important to note how Gehry differs from them. The New Minimalism is not an attempt to return to the sense of the structure as a physical presence characteristic of the American sculpture of the 1960s, which it implicitly denotes as 'old'. It is an attempt to make the look hitherto identified with Minimalist sculpture function as a representation of its former self, an iconic effect that associates the structure with self-effacement, the minimal as a convention. It is the very opposite of what Richard Serra, for instance, has always meant by Minimalism and, more pertinently, of what Gehry has made it do in his work. There is a sense, however, in which the New Minimalism is continuous with the old. Michael Fried's famous or infamous 'Art and Objecthood', an attack on Minimalism disguised as an argument about the theatrical and anti-theatrical in sculpture, described the Minimalists as making works that occupied space (got in the way) like furniture, rather than having the kind of presence one identifies with art, which seems to possess an interior or otherwise intrinsic life.[2] Fried was thinking about the works of Tony Smith, Judd and Morris—large boxes as opposed to Anthony Caro's more traditionally composed, or conceivably anti-compositional but nonetheless articulated, sculpture. He was also writing before Serra's emergence into public ubiquity, and therefore prior to the association of material emphasis with the term 'Minimalism', which results largely from his work—and which may in its turn be seen as a clarification and extension of the Minimalist sculpture of Andre by way of Ellsworth Kelly's minimal pictorialism and Jasper Johns' use of materiality as density. To see the New Minimalist architecture in the light of Fried's argument would be to say that it retains faithfully that element in Minimalist sculpture that Gehry never accepted—the inertness of which it stands accused in 'Art and Objecthood'—while exhibiting a sublime indifference to the activation of it that unites him with Serra. Molten lead thrown in the corner of a room is not like a piece of furniture, nor are four pieces of metal that are held up only by one another.

The New Minimalism seems to advance claims that are contradictory but which make it appealing from certain perspectives. In returning to a minimal, as opposed to a 'postmodern', look, it assumes a position that places it outside of the debates of past twenty years—transcending it as it were retroactively. In its treatment of Minimalism, however, it implies that it is a historical style that can no longer be present, because it is inherently past, and therefore, like all that was rather than is, can only be brought into play as representation. This position has developed within the discourse that has dominated the visual arts and architecture for the past twenty years. As the sign of, or for, evacuated presence, the New Minimalism is perhaps a perfect compromise style in that it denies life to itself in its passive-aggressive relationship to all that it addresses. Where Gehry threatened to enliven the Neues Museum, the New Minimalism could be relied upon to defer to whatever life could already be discerned there, rather than seeking to add any to it.

Gehry's attitude to the Neues—which was that there is little vitality to discern—seems to have been central to the misunderstanding that accumulated around this project. Realising that in order to carry out the programme he would have to interfere with *something*, Gehry chose the weakest building on the site, and ran up against the will to preserve everything at any cost. And this even included that which no longer existed—it is relevant that the Neues needed to be largely rebuilt in order to be preserved, since it was bombed in the Second World War. The damaged wing is the one that in Gehry's proposal is most obscured by the new bookstore and information building. Which is to say that what Gehry planned to obscure would in any case have been a facade reconstructed by him.

The Neues had a history of uncertainty before reaching its present condition. Originally a 'meeting place for art and science' that 'endeavoured to offer an artistic and scientific view of world history in chronological sequence, from prehistory to the present', it became only gradually 'an institution exclusively dedicated to art and', in consequence, to 'the early twentieth-century idea of the original'.[5] Having at first been filled with plaster casts of classical and ancient sculpture in what one may imagine as a giant necropolis of the index, or the nineteenth-century equivalent of a huge video archive, it subsequently changed course and became (by 1911) the home only of original works of art, its highly decorated interior similarly undergoing changes in accordance with fashions in curatorial ideology.

The Neues was built by Frederich August Stüler, a student of Schinkel, in 1843 to 1859. It stands between the Altes and the Pergamon—the last museum to be built (designed by Alfred Messel and finished by Ludwig Hoffman in 1930) on the Museum Island and itself conceived as an element that would bring some cohesion to the site. It faces—as the Pergamon was meant to but does not—the Dorotheenstrasse, which runs straight up to it, making it a natural point of entry. In Gehry's programme it was to have become the point of access to the whole complex. But Gehry, who has described it as a pastiche, sought to mask and reorder it in the course of integrating it into the programme.

In Gehry's proposal the entrance and central portion of the Neues is clearly visible from the street, but its wings are largely hidden by elements that complicate the lateral movement between it and the buildings flanking it. If one were to describe it pictorially, one could say that a series of gentle curves, punctuated by a black rectangle, activate the spaces between the front door of the Neues and the Pergamon and the Altes. Gehry's proposal uses curvature and lightness—the oblique and the transparent—to make engaging and digressive connections between these buildings while increasing the amount of exhibition space available to the museum. The black rectangular building houses a bookshop and information centre with galleries above; the round one a restaurant and more galleries. New exhibition space is also provided in the bridge that now connects the Neues to the Altes, which it barely touches in a gesture indicative of the extent to which Gehry wanted to leave Schinkel's masterpiece as far as possible untouched.

Gehry's programme edits the Museum Island, then, preserving the profile of the Pergamon while using glass to expand it (fig 18), and similarly leaving the Altes as intact as possible (fig 19), but containing the Neues and rephrasing the frontage so that the primary movement along it becomes a series of transitions from the Pergamon to the Altes. The transparent screens that run around the front of the buildings Gehry adds to the scheme curve towards the entrance to the Neues, or proceed out from it, in an asymmetry that is repeated by an entry arch made of curved lines. This joins the two and interpolates a slight digression between the sidewalk and the museum's

Fig. 18 Frank Gehry & Associates: Museum Island, Berlin, competition model, Phase One, Photo: Joshua White, 1994 © FOG&A

Fig. 19 Frank Gehry & Associates: Museum Island, Berlin, competition model, Phase One, Photo: Joshua White, 1994 © FOG&A

courtyard. Everything placed in front of the Neues encourages or implies movements that are serpentine or oblique. This includes the black rectilinear building, which is placed at a slight angle to the Neue's facade, so that the Museum Island complex meets the canal that runs along that side of it as a series of curving movements completed in the curving glass canopy that now encloses the space between the Pergamon's two wings, and, at the other end, by the bridge that stops just short of the Altes. Bringing the edge of the complex in line with the front of the Pergamon, whose two wings reach to the canal, Gehry's additions fill in the space between the water and the Neues with a variety of gestures that, in providing excitement that both directs and distracts attention towards the entrance, but at the same time away from it, offer an introduction to the museum that encourages the visitor to anticipate multiplicity and inventiveness instead of uniformity and derivativeness.

Themes begins to emerge, of opacity and transparency, the rectilinear and the curved, and of repetition as a principle of the extant museum countered and qualified, or one could say, embellished, by unique interstitial structures. Every one of these is a practical maximising of the space available rather than a decorative or rhetorical (not necessarily different things) effect. The fenestration and screens in front of the two buildings that Gehry has placed before the Neues create an entrance that is brought out to the street and functions at human scale, offering activity at eye level. One passes through it on one's way towards the Neues' front door. The museum complex is thus provided with an entrance approached from a straight street, so that from the distance one may glimpse the Neues through an intervening architectural grouping that links it to the street while keeping it the focus of attention.

This, more than anything else, seems to have been what alienated the jury. They preferred Grassi's programme, which does block off the Neues but 'preserves its integrity' by mimicking its plan. His addition on the Kupfergraben defers retroactively to what it blocks, so that one comes to realise that it is a replicant that comes first, thereby seeming—apparently convincingly as far as the jury was concerned—to preserve untouched that which it recontextualises. It is this passive-aggression that distinguishes the New Minimalism from the old: it takes over through a rhetoric of giving way. The old Minimalism, however subject to the charge of bombast, took responsibility for the aggressiveness implicit in putting large things in front of others.

But while Gehry may have learnt something about that too from Minimalism, his work is certainly no longer minimal, even in the sense in which it once was. In this, his development could be compared to the related case of the painter Frank Stella, who was associated with Minimalism at its inception. They have both proceeded from beginnings that were minimal if not reductive, but have subsequently not been afraid to complicate and elaborate the morphology of their work. 'Aggression' may not be the right word for what Gehry's practice offers where the New Minimalism offers passive-aggression. As noted, he wants you to be in a comfortable building, not an aggressive one—one where what you are doing will be improved, not impeded, by your sense of what the building is doing. These are the terms in which his practice opposes play to passivity, affirmation to aggression, in the interests of architecture. Gehry's will to rethink the existing programme rather than extend it through repeating its shortcomings as well as its moments of strength, and to take responsibility for that, is formed by a passion for building not monuments, but poetic structures that people can use.

Gehry's treatment of the island's museums obscures the Neues, folding it into the general plan while leaving the Pergamon and the Altes barely altered. The Pergamon's gallery space is massively increased by enclosing the space between its wings with a structure made almost exclusively out of glass, and by the glass addition that runs between it and the bookstore and information building. Raising the floor of the Pergamon, Gehry created an underworld for a museum full of artifacts from cultures in which that was an active concept, a lower gallery level that may be glimpsed from either side. His programme also called for the Pergamon Altar—the reassembled triumph of Mesopotamian archaeology that is the museum's centrepiece—to be moved from its present position, up against the gallery wall, out into the room, so it could be seen in the round: 'They've got a lot more of it that they can't use because it goes around the back', as he said to me. The door behind the altar, which is currently closed off, could now lead out to a café, to which one might repair when surfeited with Mesopotamian culture.

These, in addition to the reorientation of the Altes by way of the new bridge, were the major changes proposed in Gehry's original master plan. Most were made, then, on the canal side of the complex, where the entrance to the Neues was to have been framed by black and transparency (glass) on the left—as one faces it—and circular and wavy (as opposed to flat) opacity on the right. As Wildung notes, all museums are made readily accessible to one another by Gehry's plan—including the Bode, which, cut off from the rest by the elevated road, is connected to them by a passageway that runs along the front of the Pergamon. In regard to both the Museum Island's realignment to the city and the buildings' reorientation to one another within it, Gehry doesn't just frame the island complex but reactivates it in accordance with the programme given to him by the jury, which emphasised easy access and movement within it as primary criterion. His proposed consolidation made use of a point of access already in place, added significantly to the amount of gallery space available, not least through the addition of a transparent canopy, which left the building whose wings it joined virtually undisturbed, and was careful not only to preserve the integrity of the Altes, but to make an architectural point of seeking to do so.

Like the Pergamon's canopy, the bridge was meant to be seen to barely touch the Altes. Which is to say that, where the Pergamon and the Altes are concerned, he proposed to do a lot by clearly having tried to do very little.

In contrast to what he called Gehry's 'optimal functionality', Wildung's characterisation of the functional aspect of Grassi's programme is devastating:

> The (jury's) guideline with regard to the connecting of the individual subject areas has not been taken into consideration, there is no direct proximity of the monumental architectures, and the short walkway turns into a long and unattractive stretch.

> Functional defects can be seen in low lecture rooms in the basement, as well as in the lack of delivery areas, in restaurants and shops that are hard to reach, in dimensions that are considerably too small, and in the lack of a parking area for groups of visitors.[4]

He concludes:

> Grassi's design—which is capable of a consensus when it comes to constructing a public building for the city, since it is inconspicuous and, architecturally, unquestionably of classical simplicity—is nevertheless problematic in two respects, from a museum point of view. It subordinates the functionality to its basic stylistic idea, and thus it will be a nightmare for the client that commissioned it. And instead of writing a new chapter in the construction history of the Museum Island, it sets the old history in stone, so to speak—not on Schinkel's level, but rather with the stylistic methods of imitators, which even August Stüler, the architect of the Neues, did not surpass.[5]

Der Spiegel let its prejudices show when it termed Grassi's design 'strict' as well as 'inconspicuous'.[6] There's a difference between being strict and being unquestionably simple, classically or not. Exasperated by the fact that what it calls Gehry's 'California Pop-modern' should have met with the 'approval of museum people, whose architectural preferences normally reach back to the old Mesopotamian'[7] (as opposed, presumably, to the new Mesopotamian) *Spiegel* seems to come to the peculiar—given that journal's ideological convictions, but replete with the double standard upon which the latter depend—conclusion that Gehry is unsuitable for the Museum Island because he has proved acceptable to the business community. Having denounced Gehry's alleged postmodernism, *Spiegel* contradicts itself by quoting his remark that he hates postmodernism's recycling of historical styles—'To copy the past ... is like telling my kids there is no future'.[8] It then goes on to say that 'the enthusiasm of strict' (there it is again, and one gathers it is meant as a synonym for 'serious') 'people like insurance managers or business people [for Gehry's work] just shows how [well] they've done with the marble-brass-and-fashion splendour of today's culture and business architecture'.[9]

So here we have it. Business people support Gehry's work because it helps them make money. Cultural elitists, on the other hand, like it because they are selfish and have no respect for (explicitly) Berlin's architectural heritage and/or (implicitly) the decisions of juries: 'Wolf Dieter Dube, General Director of the State Museums, and Dietrich Wildung, Director of the Egyptian Museum, have sent an extensive list with wishes to change the winner ... They demand to adjust the entrance area (etc) [so] that nothing will be left from the first prize'.[10] But this is to say that both like it because it works. The objection, then, is that what works for trade shouldn't work for high culture. Culture may be supported by mercantilism, but it should be ritually separated from it, by, unsurprisingly, its strictness. Complaining that Gehry 'doesn't work out abstractions of right angles and mirror symmetry' (which would presumably be a 'strict' way of practising architecture), *Der Spiegel* describes his engagement with the client as 'a kind of architectural soul service. After long talks he gets out the hidden wishes of his clients and carves buildings ... which promise motion, freedom, individuality, and body heat'.[11]

The last paragraph of the *Spiegel* article is ambiguous, quoting Kurt Forster's remark about how if a person lived in a room as a fish lives in water he would be living in a Gehry house, but without explaining what would be wrong with that. It is, one gathers, the curves that caused the trouble—motion, freedom and individuality tending to disturb the strict. *Der Spiegel* saw in Gehry, but did not like, what Deleuze and Guattari described (see Chapter 1) as particularly sculptural: the body engaged in a reinvention of itself, recognisable as a transference of its terms onto literally inanimate (ie, built) forms, which have thereby become animated. The animated is the enemy of the strict, whose goal is fixity, knowledge as the power that holds things in place. In another context one would note that Sade is all about rendering the object of (experimental, speculative) desire immobile by tying her down. (As one might also talk about the triumph of a dominant perspective encapsulated by the camera's subordination of all to a single point of view, but photography's implicit sadism is mollified by our knowledge that it is the record of a fleeting instant.)

Misunderstanding, then, if it was that, may here be related to Gehry's refusal to provide an image of the fixed and the stable, but it expressed itself as objection to the fact that instead of imitating the forms already there, Gehry reframed the nineteenth century with the twentieth. Twenty-first-century Berlin would have therefore become a part of the Museum Island rather than something that happened only inside its museums or across the water from it. Where Grassi and Chippendale carefully sought to make the contemporary a discrete frame, Gehry used it as a way of rediscovering the complex and bringing to it a functionality it never had.

From that followed the rage against curvature that brought together those who wanted nothing changed out of reverence for an idea of Berlin, and those who—regardless of what they thought about conservation—were New Minimalists and as such did not like curves. The opposition of the first group became stronger than misunderstanding with regard to Gehry's feeling that the Neues should become essentially a transitional area upon whose visual grandeur the visitor would be unlikely to pause. Gehry's recognition that this building is less interesting than those surrounding it, and that it makes a weak link between them, involved a value judgement unpalatable *prime facie*. Gehry shifted the entry point to the complex by making use of the street that runs at an axis to the Neues, but saw that something new needed to happen at the point where they meet. No-one else wanted anything to take place that would disturb what is happening there already, which is not much.

As opposition to his proposal consolidated in what was described earlier as the second stage of his involvement with this project, Gehry did come up with non-curvy solutions to this question. When the project withered to a mild reform of the Neues, plus a couple of other elements, he revised the bridge to the Altes twice, ending up with one that resembles something from an airport, or possibly recalls Walter Gropius' Bauhaus building in Dessau. But by that time, the opportunity truly to integrate the site into Berlin as it now is had been withdrawn. When recalled to propose a plan specifically for the Neues, he offered a reform of the interior, which foundered once again on what is perceived as his lack of regard for the intrinsics of the building as it is. From Gehry's point of view, it is not a lack of regard but the opposite: a recognition of the need to supplement what he perceives as a lack. One may make it better, but not by leaving it as it is. Wild horses, he says, could not drag him back to this project. Everything he put forward was based on an idea of the urban as a meeting of the historical and the actual, in a situation encumbered by a reverence for history that proved stifling.

This returns us to Wildung's description of Gehry's programme as preserving the dignity of the buildings, bringing them together while critically realising the teleological potential of their juxtaposition. It is in these terms that the Museum Island project and its reception raise questions about public architecture that are also questions about Berlin and how it wants to reconstitute itself in the wake of reunification, for these are what converge in a description of what Wildung calls this project's 'spectacularity'. Few seem to disagree with Wildung's estimate of the superiority of Gehry's programme as the one that made the most sense for Museum Island considered as an architectural context for displaying works of art and other cultural artifacts. It was what was to go on the outside that caused most of the trouble. The spectacularity of the art display was one thing; the spectacle of the Museum Island as a confirmation that Germany's past (or pasts, for there are more than one), is not straightforwardly continuous with its present—history involves criticism and is not a matter of eternal verities—quite another. To repeat, what was at stake in this project was the integration of the Museum Island into Berlin as it is now—a city reinventing itself. Gehry's project was about nothing less than how Berlin wants to represent itself to itself: how it wants to think its present, and that present's connections to and disconnections from its various pasts; and presumably, what this relating of the present to its pasts implies for a future (at the level of aspiration rather than prediction, since one is talking here of values put forward, or advertised, by a symbolic order).

Any national museum is bound to induce mixed feelings. When in the British Museum, for example, one is the beneficiary of earlier generations' proclivity for theft. One cannot visit Museum Island without some thought about the relationship between German history and the idea of culture. Schinkel and the Prussian state, the colonisation of history by German archaeology in the Pergamon, are among the connotations and associations that come to mind when one is there. Both lead to Hegel and his provocatively titled *The Philosophy of History*. Bearing in mind the contemptuous attitude to Europe as a whole attributed to him by *Der Spiegel*, for example, I think it worth saying, before going any further, that Gehry has never been guilty of conventional stupidity with respect to German culture and its history. One might point by way of an example to his building for the DG Bank Building (completed 2000)—approved by the same officials who found the Museum Island unacceptable—close by at 3 Pariser Platz, next to the Brandenberg Gate. It contains a form reminiscent of a large horse's head whose invocations of Teutonic symbology brought him reproach from vulgar pietists who believe of Germany what they would not believe of any other nation, namely that its culture led to one thing only, and as such should be either expunged or preserved solely as expiation and apology.

Hegel saw Germany as having survived being 'traversed'[12]—as he politely puts it—by the French, thanks to the nationalism that Bonaparte's traversal induced. But it is the international side of Germany's contribution to cultural history that visiting the Museum Island brings to mind today. It is not that the history of Europe existed to culminate in the Prussian state, but that the museum's systematic arrangement of art objects so that they culminated in something was a Hegelian achievement, first tried out by Schinkel in the Altes Museum, which was to define the discipline. The teleology of culmination may have changed and even become a question of the provisional and the unanticipated, but Europe's (and perhaps the world's) visual culture long ago became part of what was originally a German intellectual project called Art History, predicated on the belief that the history of objects revealed the purpose of history itself. In this sense, when on Museum Island one feels oneself to be at a centre and origin of museum culture. The 'spectacle' would, then, be one of museum culture. The accusation levelled against Gehry's proposal was that it aimed at a spectacle of the kind provided by Walt Disney's commercial heirs, a Museumland, or Cultureworld.

Gehry's proposal threatened nothing of the sort, except to the extent that the programme called for large numbers of people to enjoy visiting the museums. The comparison with other forms of mass entertainment raises the question of what would, in practice, be wrong with that? As far as I know, tourists visiting the Louvre do not see it as exactly the same kind of experience as a visit to Euro Disney, but why should it cause dismay if a child were to do so? Where do purists see the rot as first setting in? Is it when the gift shop starts to sell t-shirts as well as postcards, or earlier, when posters appear around town and on public transport suggesting that a visit to the museum might be enjoyable? Nor is this a contemporary issue. It was not a contemporary museum, but the Victoria and Albert, of which Queen Mary remarked: 'Wonderful, charming, such a pity, don't you think, that everything looks as though it's for sale?'.[13] Given that she presided over an overwhelmingly mercantile culture, her sentiment is suggestive as well as snotty. *Der Spiegel*, as we have seen, agrees with her in wanting art to be kept apart from the presentational techniques common in commercial life. Victorian advertising and commercial display were gaudy, which is to say, not strict. The Victorian museum displayed things with an emphasis on profusion that matched the department store's investment in the same principle. The contemporary museum is similarly obliged to prove itself capable of being as entertaining as anything else to which the middle-class family might want to visit. When it doesn't, it signals the absence of a levity that for *Der Spiegel* and Queen Mary means vulgarity.

The opposition to Gehry's proposal had a great deal to do with his introduction of what were perceived as signs of an inadmissible levity, represented by the lack of right-angles, into the image of museum culture on the one hand and the city of Berlin on the other. The association of curvature with levity adds doubt about internationalism to an impoverished concept of the serious. Internationalism nowadays means international capitalism—mercantilism that weakens nationalism. If one associates curvature in architecture, not to say elsewhere, with not being strict—the strict and the not-curved were how eighteenth-century aesthetics defined the masculine as opposed to the feminine—one associates it more immediately with mobility. With regard to buildings, it is then a short step to recognising that the curves ones sees in contemporary buildings are made possible by a technology that represents in itself an unprecedented cultural condition.

If museum culture is internationally representative of, indebted to, and derived from, a German model, then to visit a German museum is to enter a culture that is internationalised—just as to engage 'English' literature is not to engage only works written by the English. There is, then, no intrinsic reason why local characteristics or references need to be monumentalised or otherwise presented by museums. We slip instead into something already conventionalised in the nineteenth century, where the museum signified itself by suggesting the Greeks or the Romans, like the National Gallery in London or the Metropolitan Museum in New York, but with an important difference. The nineteenth century knew what culture was: JJ Winckelmann had established its stages and a feasible stylistic genealogy, albeit on the basis of misattributions. Hegel established its development and, for some, its teleology. However, in the late twentieth century, it is the thrill of the speculative that energises culture, whereas the ecstasy of the ideal motivated its acolytes in the past. It would seem to be important, then, that whatever it looked like, the museum would nowadays need to present its contents in something other than an order that had about it an aura of inevitability. The only way to do this is to make the place comfortable as a space in which people may feel free to play, which in a museum means feeling free to have an idea of one's own. Such a programme would, as Gehry's did, tend to substitute convergence, coincidence and digression for a traditional orientation towards the unidirectional.

With regard to which one would also say that while Berlin—as the capital of northern central Europe—faces both West and East, it now finds itself in a world that has long since ceased to be securely spatial, whose internationalism is predicated on the collapse of space and therefore time into simultaneity, and where divergence and convergence are characteristic of a capitalism without a centre. This is the world within which the reunification of Germany is taking place, and it raises the question of how to think about the present, given that while one may be able to blame Bismarck for the Third Reich, and by extension for Germany's post-war division, he cannot be held responsible for the new Berlin, an unanticipated effect of the unexpected, or at best (in practice, worst), premature, collapse of the Soviet Union.

Berlin, then, simultaneously faces a question about how suddenly to become a capital city again, and another about what kind of a centre a capital city should be when it functions within a decentred capitalism in which capital moves around the world at will, demonstrating as it does the anachronicity of the nation state and national culture. The controversy over the Museum Island project is part of the issue of whether the reunification of Berlin—and of Germany as a whole—should take place in terms of the new, or in terms of the old, reaching back beyond the occupation and the Hitler years to an earlier, 'original', Berlin, which will be realised (ie, simulated, represented, as opposed to presented for the first time) as the originary Berlin. The new Berlin is no more, or less, irreducibly German or Prussian or Berlin-ish than London is irreducibly English or New York is American. All cities have now been eaten away by an internationalism that they engendered; all metropoles prefigure the cosmopolis. The Museum Island project takes place in a museum culture that is international while having once been German, and within an international culture that Berlin has no more ability to evade or resist than does anywhere else. All resistance, however worthwhile, will only be experienced as temporary and symbolic. Berlin may pass ordinances that preserve the outline of the local architectural tradition, but the outline is filled in by Burger King and The Gap there as everywhere else. Capitalism is itself nomadic and has consumed the last nomads. The cattle herds of Deleuze's Mongolians, treasured image of that which the urban, the metropole, keeps at a distance but cannot regulate because it knows its own lines of flight, are now under exclusive contract to McDonald's for the Chinese market.

No city can resist such a force, but any city can choose how it will relate to it. It's the question of what to do with the nineteenth century and its antecedents and consequences, among which last is the world as it is now. All over the capitalist world, cities are built around stranded and supplemented elements of nineteenth-century grandeur, built to last and still lasting, that contain the past and knowledge in general. Many, if not most, great Western museums are nineteenth-century shells whose contents have been augmented and rearranged to suit the palette of the general public— conceivably, but in practice, infrequently, people who might as soon go to Disneyland as to a museum. They are also modified to reflect the doubts about nineteenth-century triumphalism that, being characteristic of contemporary thought, are shared by the people who work there. The curators who work in major museums, presenting the world to itself through their organisation of its artifacts, work in nineteenth-century buildings while being professionally engaged in reconsidering that century's aspirations and assumptions.

One is, then, used to seeing art and other traces of cultural production, from whatever period, including this one, in an inherently anachronistic setting, and accustomed to that anachronism being nineteenth, and less often, eighteenth century. The Victoria and Albert Museum, the Science Museum, etc, in Knightsbridge in London, make up a varied and fabulous assortment of knowledge presentations, all nineteenth-century, and all thus engaged in rearrangement of a paradigm within buildings whose facades preserve the attitudes reordered within them by historical and cultural criticism, but to which they are immutably impervious.[14] Gehry's Museum Island project addressed that immutability from outside as well as from within, by giving interiors and exteriors new things to do. In the case of the best of the latter, this followed from Gehry's willingness to rethink its physical connection to the city. The present condition of the Altes Museum recalls Wildung's remarks about preserving extant dignity more strongly than any other part of the site, and this is precisely because it is so hard to approach it as it was meant to be approached.

The Altes is an image of the stranded past in its purest form, the vista that it faces changed by history and in particular filled with vehicular traffic.

This feeling of the stranded is emphasised nowadays by one's never having seen the Altes as it was meant to be seen. Until recently at least, one crossed the great open space to be immediately blocked by plastic sheeting and directed to the right or left, depending on whether or not one was going to hang up one's coat once one had entered the building. That was a temporary condition, but the strandedness of the prospect on which it gazes is not. The question for Gehry was, then: how does one use it while preserving it; and what is the dignity that one wants to preserve?

Gehry's answer was to transform it from the way into the museum to the space outside it. In the sense that this allowed for a more efficient use of the building's interior, and followed logically from the adaptation of the Neues Museum into an entrance to the Museum Island as a whole, it was a solution that derived from the exigencies of the programme. But it would have been the right solution even if it had been arrived at by another route. It permits Schinkel's museum to preserve its own space. By no longer letting that area function quite as it once did, Gehry allows us to rediscover it, its proportions, its calm and the possibility of distancing oneself from the building in order to see it. We do not perceive it as truncated, because Gehry has offered a way in which its discontinuity with its context, partly a product of the twentieth century, partly of its manifest superiority as architecture, may be made to work *as* discontinuity rather than as a sign of that which once was, or might have been.

The dignity that Gehry's proposal preserved was the idea of place put forward by the architecture. Like the Disney Music Hall, which will be discussed in the following chapter, detachment ends up being a way towards reattachment. Schinkel's museum is transformed from a sign for the incomplete—a symptom of a now defunct gaze, designed for a panorama that long since gave way to quite another—into a space for a different kind of looking: one of critical reflection. The museum's courtyard is no longer about commanding a vista, or about distancing the building from anything save the viewer who wants to see its facade as a whole, which is to say, it has become a frame for the building rather than the path towards it. Gehry has made the courtyard into a reflection of the museum's space, an expression of the amount of room the museum requires in order to be seen, by turning it into a site one may enter by leaving the museum rather than the only way into it. What has been abolished? The pathos of the museum as it is, where the effect of stranded grandeur is exacerbated by the courtyard as one further detail in a somewhat awkward access, which involves crossing streets or coming upon it from the side, so that it reads as a culmination where everything that led up to it has been lost.

Elsewhere in the project, as noted, every element that Gehry has added to the Museum Island announces itself as such—ie, as an addition that is also a framing—which returns one to the question of curvature. The idea of transitionality as a function of framing is underscored by the use of a black cube for the bookstore and information centre building, which stands in contrast to the other additions that surround it. It anchors the movements created on either side of it by glass and curvature, while its rectilinearity relates directly to the Neues, whose wings it equals in height, but which, as remarked above, it does not parallel, being instead placed at a slight angle to it, so that it comes out towards the canal or leads back towards the entrance like the round restaurant building next to it.

Gehry places another kind of motion in tension with what is already there—in doing so giving new emphasis to the dome on the top of the Bode, sundry roof details on the Altes and the Neues, and the curving colonnade around the National Gallery. The latter would have been diametrically opposed to the bridge that Gehry planned between the Neues and the Altes— so that the colonnade would have been on one's right as one looked at the National Gallery from the river, and Gehry's bridge on one's right as one looked at the site from the canal. Where Grassi's design paralleled the existing structures, 'mickey-moused' them as they'd say in Hollywood, Gehry chose to preserve the buildings' integrity by framing them with something clearly other than themselves.

As has been said: 'In contrast [to Gehry's programme] the project drawn up by Grassi, with new structures rendered in a language reminiscent of the utilitarian architecture used by Schinkel for the Customs facilities that previously stood on the spot, seemed a discretion bordering on self-abnegation'.[15] This comparison of Grassi's 'self-abnegation' with Schinkel's utilitarianism—another word for 'practicality'—deserves a little attention *en passant*. The distinction is between Schinkel's epoch, in which the undecorated was not a style so much as that which lay outside of architecture as high art, ie, outside of the question of style, and Grassi's, in which that which lies outside of the question of style *is* a style. That is the sense, discussed above, in which one would characterise New Minimalism's 'self-abnegation' as passive-aggressive: it is less self-abnegation than the assertion of self-abnegation as a dominant style, which gives way to all others in order to bring them together. It creates a whole in which hitherto independent entities become subordinate to that which appears to defer to them. (This may be what the author means when he describes it as 'bordering' on self-abnegation rather than being it.) Regardless of how one feels about it, it seems tendentious to claim continuity between such a deployment of the look of a style-less style in the late twentieth century and an earlier utilitarianism. It is, on the contrary, the 'look' of the utilitarian, without any more utilitarianism than one may find in any other way of working—it is neither cheaper nor more functional. One is reminded of Gehry's observation about the inapplicability of the idea of 'truth to materials' in a world where one can build anything. In such a world, no architecture is any more utilitarian than any other. And if one is to say that the very notion appeals to the distinction between architecture and building that has fuelled so much architectural discourse, then one may say that either may be as practical as the other. The distinction dissolves in an age where art is generally required to be anti-art in order to become art, and architecture, in parallel, frequently becomes architecture by deploying the counter-idea of building. The curators who found Grassi's programme unacceptable seem to have discovered this for themselves.

What Gehry offered instead of a stylistics of self-effacement was a solution that opens the site up to other kinds of movement that are neither alien—they are inherent in the site—nor familiar—they don't immediately seem to derive from the existing structures even when they do—that leave the buildings as untouched by their contemporary context as possible, while still connecting them to it. It is true that in linking them to the twentieth century, the plan acknowledges that their place in it is a little different from what it might have been in the nineteenth. The idea of culture, for example, is not what it was for Hegel. Nor, without wanting to attribute to positions like those taken by the New Minimalists an innocence of which they may not be entirely guilty, is the distinction between cultural production then and now one between an unreflective notion of culture and one that is self-critical. Culture was already being made out of self-criticism (ie was Hegelian) when Schinkel built the Altes. The issue is rather that if architecture is made in part out of critical reflection on what culture once was and can no longer plausibly be—for example, triumphalist and teleologically certain—that reflection can only be productive (as opposed to exclusively critical, or destructive) to the extent that it provides the grounds for a determination of what it might be instead, not only by default but also as the result of a desire to recognise what has happened.[16] For example, to be productive, it would want to take into account what the internationalisation of culture by capitalism makes available as well as—but also because of—what it does to the past.

Gehry's additions are as discrete as their internal logic permits, but in expanding the available space, they caused a fuss because they altered a familiar and identifying element in the Berlin skyline—there are limits to discretion if one is doubling something's size. The complaint, then, had less to do with the site and the buildings on it than with the Museum Island's function as a historico-cultural icon within a city considered as a skyline made up of signs for Berlin as entity and idea.

Given his overt and longstanding interest in architecture's relationship to the idea of the social, it remains unclear why anyone more informed than, say, a journalist running up a quick and surly little number for *Der Spiegel* would suppose that Gehry was not sensitive to such issues as these. His plan changes the skyline in the course of restoring the site, preserving the architecture while recognising that cities change, not least because of technology. Gehry's proposal was provocative because it suggested that the time has come for a new kind of movement to play its part in the city's visual sense of itself. Had it been adopted, the Museum Island would have become an active component in a skyline otherwise changing around it, able to function as an index of the present rather than an icon of the (symbolically) unchanging.

Berlin's government has determined that buildings will not be too high, and that their distance from the street will continue to be uniform. This suggests a certain kind of look that may indeed be so fundamental to an idea of Berlin treasured by its inhabitants that no one would wish it to disappear. However, it returns one to the question of the rest of the world, and to the techno-capitalist environment that Berlin shares with it. There is a sense in which Berlin seems to be trying to keep the rest of the world indoors: inside, one may be cosmopolitan to an extent that is precluded on the street, as it were. One of the most exciting architectural environments in contemporary Berlin is the inside of the new Galeries Lafayette shop on Franzosischstrasse (designed by Jean Nouvel, Emmanuel Cattani & Associates, 1996)—not that far from Museum Island—where floors have been arranged around a circular opening that reaches from roof to basement, widening towards the top, and thus permitting commercialism to attach itself to a mildly agoraphobic or vertiginous thrill. Being inside it increases one's sense that the form and movement described and proposed by the opening would not be permitted in Berlin were it the shape of a building's exterior.

This cannot be an entirely satisfactory policy. It suggests too strongly that, while Berlin may be able to resist the lunacy of historical areas that are restored to a state that is more like they were than they ever were—as in the plan to put cobblestones on the streets of New York's SoHo district, which never had them—it wants to impose a curious kind of restriction on thinking visually about itself. Those in charge seem to be saying that whatever culture (political, economic, or technological) does, if it does it in Berlin it will adjust itself to a model that is not to be questioned, despite having a specific historical origin. To Americans, this will be reminiscent of the reverence for the US Constitution, similarly of a particular moment but now officially timeless, which may guard against some extreme barbarities but also long ago became a mechanism for keeping an economic order in place rather than facilitating social change. Reverence for Schinkel's vision of Berlin, if that is what is at issue here, could similarly guard against the worst, while serving primarily only to resist productive change by policing the symbolic. Given the Hegelian flavour of it all, it seems even more absurd that such a view could prevail when the Museum Island itself contains Schinkel as both himself and as farce.

That is what requires reconciliation, together with the disproportion between the Pergamon and the other museums, and where logic led to emphasising the latter in regard to the former. it suggested amelioration and revision. It is absurd to repeat farce as farce, which is to say, one can't preserve a bad building in the same way one preserves a good one. Gehry's plan gave the Neues Museum a purpose: 'We were clearing it and making it into a great hall... to rebuild a pastiche of a pastiche goes to the other problem'. The other problem being that to rebuild exactly as it was something that should never have been built that way in the first place would be to maintain the unfortunate relationship between the Neues and the Altes that currently exists. That said, one wonders what would be frozen in place were the current silhouette of the complex preserved intact.

Gehry's proposal for the rehabilitation of the Museum Island allowed its buildings to reach out towards the present while preserving them, but not indiscriminately and indecisively. There is a price to pay for making things better, as one might say. Gehry's programme introduced movements other than the constant pace of the grid into the site, in so doing rediscovering aspects of what is already there and finding a new use for them. *Inter alia*, the curvature introduced by Gehry reduced the severity of the rectilinear, proposing ambling instead of marching, fluidity instead of motion made out of repeated units. Although none of those who complained about what the project would do to Berlin's skyline seemed in any way aware of it, Gehry had internalised into the design a reference to the Spree and the canal, to the water on three sides of the Museum Island. The undulation and variety of Gehry's new buildings along the Kupfergraben (figs 8–11, above) adjusts the Pergamon and the Altes to the pace of the river, like that of the museum visitor, an unmechanical movement within an environment of the built and the engineered. The river that runs through Berlin is an important part of its identity, one might have thought, and there is no reason why it shouldn't play a part in one's experience of the museum's locale. It seems as though a preoccupation with how the buildings look from afar might have obscured what was adjacent to them. Or was it that, for the city fathers concerned to achieve change while leaving things exactly as they are, any kind of movement that isn't regulated by the grid is unacceptable? If so, that would be another sign of resistance to the contemporary.

If it leads to the natural movement of water, curvature also leads to its opposite and derivative—technology. In the Galeries Lafayette it joins the body with techno-capitalism in a thoroughly satisfying manner, causing easy transition from lingerie to *lindzertorte* in a curving world that connects one sense to another coherently and without interruption, as Merleau-Ponty said it should. At the most banal level, to refuse curvature in architecture of the sort Gehry put forward in the Museum Island proposal is to refuse contemporary building technology.

What seems to be involved, once one puts it like that, is a social and democratic crisis with which one could in principle have some sympathy. It certainly leads to the question of preservation. The idea seems to be that nineteenth-century models of the eternal can survive unscathed, regardless of how the world changes, and the way things in it are built. But rather than remaining as touchstones in a world of change, forms that have become implicitly, if not explicitly, outmoded become stranded, and a civic-aesthetic administrative regime that insists it will literally contain change by not permitting fundamental alterations in exterior form—change will only happen on the inside—is insisting far too forcefully. The idea of using historical forms to fend off history implies a use for them at odds with their original purpose, and, given that Schinkel's ghost is at the centre of the dispute, bizarrely so, since everything about them would inevitably be altered by their being reapplied as models for an age not their own. They anticipate the present only retrospectively, and this new-found responsibility for that which they never knew would be bound to subject them to stress and strain.

Gehry, on the other hand, proposed an adjustment of the Berlin skyline that began to relate the city to a world that has moved beyond the grid (albeit through being a confusion of grids), characterised by another kind of body, and manifested in an architecture that has no innate dependence on cubes and cylinders. In Gehry's proposal for Museum Island, contemporary technology (which has dissolved the mechanical's Gordian gridlock into electronic flows), offered to frame and preserve the original buildings by not pretending continuity with them save at the level of the programme. Which is to say, it was continuous with them in being founded in an idea about who was going to use the building and for what—a continuity that could only be achieved by recognising that neither are now quite what they once were. One returns to Gehry's discretion regarding mediocrity. All cities have buildings that are not all that good but which the inhabitants nonetheless love; there is little evidence, however, that the citizens of Berlin are united in a sentimental attachment to the Neues Museum. Gehry's plan brought it into a far more comfortable relationship with those buildings to which it is adjacent, especially Schinkel's. As always with Gehry, attention was focused on his proposal's radicality. It would have been better to see it as one that initially made a clear break between addition and what was already there, but after that, worked in terms of intensification and softening rather than of replacement.

The glass canopy over what is now the space between the two wings of the Pergamon is a case in point. As noted, the programme required that the museums handle a number of visitors far greater than their original architects or programmes anticipated, which necessitated some filling in and opening up. Gehry converted an exterior to an interior space without doing anything to the buildings except to join them with a generalised echo, not of their shape, but of the movement between them, a shallow arch that it is easy to relate to the movement of the head as one looks from one to the other. Everywhere one goes in this design, one is struck by its subtlety, providing that one first accepts that it is built out of materials available now. When Gehry was asked whether he thought, *a propos* the Bilbao project, there was a danger of the architecture overpowering the art, he said he wasn't worried about it because that is not what his buildings do.[17] It might equally be said that there was never any prospect of the Altes or the Pergamon being overpowered, and Gehry's almost total preservation of their exteriors confirm that he never intended that they should be.

When Gehry says his architecture doesn't overpower the art it contains, he means that it is designed to release the potential of what it contains or presents, not to obscure it. In Bilbao, the architecture gives way to the art once one reaches the galleries. In Berlin, his programme linked buildings without robbing them of their individuality. But he makes things work through contemporary materials and the forms they permit, and, in that these allow Gehry to take architecture beyond a world known through an instituted certainty, it was what they represented that lay at the heart of the resistance to the Museum Island redevelopment project. Sometimes, Gehry has made indeterminacy the programme's theme. He has, for example, said of the house he designed in 1996 for Jay Chiat in Telluride that 'Jay's house went for indeterminacy' (it is still unbuilt, the client responding to the indeterminate with indecision). Indeterminacy, by definition that which slips through or never needed the grid, is characteristic of the techno-capitalism in which—in practice if not symbolically—Berlin finds itself at the end of the twentieth century. Gehry's use of the materials and procedures that contemporary technology makes possible allows him to bring it into his work. However, what these forms make possible was overlooked by a critique of their connotations. Rather than seeing what it did, his opponents saw his proposal only as an image they didn't like.

Gehry always works with two models, one large for the building, another on a smaller scale that allows him to keep his eye on its relationship to its context. Both change as the idea progresses, which is to say, change comes from within both. This is a method of working within which development takes place through mutual deferral. It is one of the practical expressions of the more general sense in which Gehry inverts Heidegger and lives comfortably, which is to say, inventively, in the world of the deferred but simultaneous—things deferring to their identity as signs, time as distance abolished by the telephone—of bodies detached from experience by that combination of deferral and simultaneity but constantly reattached through reference to movement that is not that of the grid. The grid expresses an older, humanist model of capitalist democracy, based on modularity and repetition rather than the electronic pulse and flow that defines the techno-capitalism we have now—cause and effect rather than immediacy and the event. The grid is also the regime of the same as opposed to a field of singularities. It is in the light of that distinction that one might think of the glass roof that Gehry added to the Pergamon as a use of transparency to enclose a volume while preserving its original identity as a negative space; of his use of curvature as a framing that softens but also speeds up the connection between the forms it joins; and of the black cube that he placed in front of the Neues as an intensification through contrast or inversion of what elsewhere are all additions that add movement while the cube acts as concentration and fulcrum.

Deleuze has been mentioned here already, and one may recall what he had to say with regard to the fold, and with reference to capitalism's triumph through weakness (its ability to fold into its system even the nomads, by resisting nothing), to the body that finds itself in other forms (which are not forms but activities and ways of being) and to liquidity and its further condition, the gaseous.[18] Gehry's interest in liquidity came out of, or was first manifested in, the body that lives in bodies of water: the fish. Fish are streamlined, but it is more to the point that they have scales, an articulated surface. Gehry's World Exposition Amphitheatre (built and then disassembled, 1994) was an early expression of this idea. Of the unbuilt Samsung Museum of Modern Art in Seoul (design began in 1995, work continued until 1997) he himself has said that it 'got to liquid'. In other words, he managed to make structure become fully active as more than an expression of a skeleton.[19] Fluidity provides a surface that limits a depth but makes it impossible to tell where one begins and the other ends because there is no outside skin, while the same movement runs through the whole—possibly slower in the depths than above. The passage is from scales—the surface that has many movements—to fluid—movement without repetition or parts, but capable of different speeds, which is to say, made not of separate spaces but containing different times.

The fish evolved to live in water; it is never apart from it and it never gets lost in it, except when it wants to. It cannot be apart from it, and therefore cannot possibly experience itself as wet. It lives fluidity by living in it. Gehry has similarly sought to drive architecture towards a condition of continuity with its context that forces the solid into a relationship with movement that has weight as water has weight and is at the same time lighter than air. In this condition, one might experience the body and embodiment—for example, skin or surface, the whole as that which knows itself as both complete and infinitely in need of supplementation, including through reflection—as mobilities, provisional, speculative, not bound by the finitude of their identity as solids. Instead it is mobilised by the potential offered by dissolution or evaporation considered as active states. On more than one occasion, Deleuze has divided philosophy and therefore thought in general into the solid, the fluid, and the gaseous—three conditions of bodies, bone, blood, air—skin something between solid and fluid, at once articulated but continuous. In his book on cinema, he begins by attributing different properties of solidity, fluidity and gaseousness to different cinematic genres. Gehry and Deleuze do not allow the body to be solid for very long on any given occasion, and one notes that there may be fluid or gaseous movement, whereas movements with solidity, or made by it, draw on the other two for analogy or inspiration. In Gehry's Museum Island project, fluidity envelops, with an almost gaseous discretion, ethereal in the sense of a cloud, a solidity that it represents to its best effect in the cases of the Altes and the Pergamon, and to which it lends needed supplementation in that of the Neues. At the same time, like a fish, it takes its form from the flow in which it swims: the contemporary city and the things out of which it is built.

One might say that the most obvious basis for comparing Gehry's thinking with Deleuze's is that in Deleuze, the body is never there as a whole, but as a possibility constituted by a meeting between outsides, a contextual event irreducible to its causes and effects but involving an act of recognition. In Gehry's Museum Island, a number of outsides meet one another, what brings them together finding itself in the order that is already there, itself rediscovered (re-cognised) in the possibilities that arise from what reunites it. Given that these are cultural institutions that need to find a new way of working with the help of contemporary technology, there would have to be an allegorical dimension to the programme's solution. How culture is presented tells a story about the context within which the presentation is taking place. Germany's reunification ran out of money, and so has Museum Island's reunification, which followed from it and has similarly receded into piecemeal gestures, collectively amounting to a tableau depicting symbolic resistance to the present that, regrettably, signifies only a fear of being overwhelmed by it. As an allegory of the symbolic administration of socio-cultural life, it is about that most Hegelian concept, the spirit of the age, administered here not by those who curate cultural artifacts but by those who administer the curators. Gehry's solution to the programme linked, through an attitude to preservation that maximised what was there while supplementing what was not and never had been, the buildings on Museum Island to that outside that is (always) already inside: the contemporary as a material condition, around but already within each of the buildings in the complex, and around, but thoroughly pervasive in, the city of Berlin. Not the Berlin that should have been, either then or now, but the one that actually is: a messy Berlin, uncertain about how long it can keep its buildings low. The Berlin that is the capital city of the reunified Germany that actually is, and that exists within a Europe engaged in a perpetual, but inexorable, quest to turn itself into a Community. The material condition of Berlin consists of more than one system, and traversing all of them is the one that changes everything everywhere: the technology of everyday contemporary life. This is also an everyday ideology that washes away distinctions between, for example, national identities and cultural forms— which are only ever hybrids—while bringing others—of a post-national hybridity—into view. In Gehry's proposal, one set of ideas did not have to kill another; each could, instead, have enlivened the other through a play of historical continuity and the specifics of Berlin's present.

Notes

1. Dietrich Wildung, 'Die Qual der Wahl, Zum Architektenwettbewerb "Museminsel Berlin"' ('The Agony of Making a Decision: The Architectural Competition for the Museum Island in Berlin'), *Antike Welt*, XXV, 2, 1994, pp 119–20.
2. Michael Fried, 'Art and Objecthood', 1967, in G Battcock (ed), *Minimal Art*, EP Dutton, New York, 1968.
3. Kaye Geipel, 'Restoring a Torso: Neues Museum, Berlin', *AV Monografías 71*, Madrid, 1988, p 99.
4. Wildung, op cit.
5. Ibid.
6. 'Sonnen-Pop im Nebelland' ('Sun Pop in the Hazyland'), *Der Speigel*, XXXVIII, 1994, pp 200–203.
7. Ibid.
8. Ibid.
9. Ibid.
10. Ibid.
11. Ibid.
12. GWF Hegel, *The Philosophy of History*, trans J Sibree, Prometheus Books, Buffalo, New York, 1991, p 455.
13. Kurt W. Forster, 'Shrine? Emporium? Theater' Reflections on Two Decades of American Museum Building', *Zodiac 6*, Milan, March–April 1991, p 42.
14. When, or if, Daniel Libeskind's extension to the V & A is completed, London will have two examples of how to add on while preserving the original buildings virtually intact. The V & A extension will be different in every obvious way from the building it supplements, in contrast to the National Gallery's Sainsbury wing (Venturi, Scott, Crown & Associates, 1991), which, because of the distance between its entrance and the old one, has a far more discrete relationship to it: a sharp distinction between the past and the present in the V & A, and a barely perceptible one in the NG. The relevance of either programme to the project under discussion here is, however, limited. Neither the NG nor the V & A were dilapidated, part of an incoherent complex, nor poorly situated with regard to access from the street.
15. Geipel, op cit, p 101
16. This question also returns one to Gehry's sense of the social function of architecture. After this book was written, he and I had supper and, talking about something else for once, discovered that we both read and reread Anthony Trollope. Gehry described a party in Trollope's *The Warden* (1855) Chap X, "The Warden's Tea Party" which he said could be seen, in the relationships and personalities it involved, to provide a model of the city. I myself was reminded of the famous conflict in

Barchester Towers (1857) between Archdeacon Grantly and Bishop Proudy, or more precisely, the latter's wife. It is a High Church/Low Church conflict, and Trollope perversely demonstrates that it is the High Church that is more inclusive, in practice if not in principal (Trollope's heroes tend to be Tories while he himself ran for Parliament as a Liberal). Grantly's position is that one should have as few sermons as possible, on the grounds that they are divisive because they bring up socially disruptive topics. Instead, he advocates sermons that are brief and general, so that there's a minimum amount of sermonizing and a maximum of time spent on activities in which every one can join and, incidentally as it were, each have a place. The alternative is to devote a maximum amount of time to preaching, during which the congregation is reminded why it is good that they are there and why true enjoyment comes from not enjoying oneself. One could make a comparison between these ecclesiastical differences and those between a building in which there's a lot to do, and one in which one may only admire the architectural programme. This is especially so when, as is the case with official postmodernism, to admire is to revel in negation, guaranteeing a shared delusion of (implicitly pious) superiority by making criticality the point of the experience.

17. Interview on TELVA, 1997.
18. Gilles Deleuze, *Cinema 1: the Movement Image*, trans Hugh Tomlinson and Barbara Habberjam, University of Minnesota Press, Minneapolis, 1986, pp 76–86.
19. Work on the design for the Samsung Museum of Modern Art came to an end when the client withdrew in the course of the financial disarray which transformed the Asian economies from miracles to debacles toward the end of 1997. The client had in any case not been able to secure the whole site, part of which was bought by Samsung's chief rival while the planning was going on, and the museum has now merged with another in order exhibit its collection.

CHAPTER 3
Los Angeles: Music and the Idea of the Centre

I can do a jiggly-wiggly and build it and it'll look like that. No-one else
can do that. Except Corbu. Corbu could do that.

In Berlin, Gehry sought to bring an idea and experience of the museum
together with the city as it is—or will be in the immediate future when the
scaffolding comes off all that's being built at the time of writing—and ran
afoul of a German sense that art should be joyful but not too much fun. As
one might say, there's a levity limit. In Los Angeles, he had other problems.
These, alas, were not simply the reverse of the Berlin ones—he has never
been accused of not providing enough fun—but rather, their inverse. They
belonged to discourses and incidents altogether external and indifferent to
the aesthetic, however conceived or deployed. As with the Berlin project,
where the objections were decisive but had nothing to do with the
programme, the infuriating circumstances and accidentally beneficial
consequences of the Walt Disney Concert Hall's prolonged evolution had
nothing to do with its function as a place for the performance of music. But
it is that which is most important here. Music has had as much influence on
the way Gehry works as have the visual arts or the experience of living in
Los Angeles, and the Disney Concert Hall's programme is founded on his
thinking about music and the listener. It may also be significant that where
Gehry has been involved with both contemporary and historical art and
contemporary and classical music, he has had more to do with contemporary
than historical art but the opposite is true of music. Perhaps this means that
he finds immediacy in the visual arts but complexity in music—the bluntness
of Minimalism, but realised as a symphony rather than preserved as a
reduction.

I listened with interest, early in the Disney Concert Hall project's
development, to Gehry discussing the merits and deficiencies of the acoustics
of the (many) concert halls with which he was familiar. He had toured the
world's auditoria with the committee that chose him to build the Disney Hall,
along with members of the orchestra that will play in it. (Much later, Richard
Koshalek, part of that committee, would tell me that both the committee and
the musicians had listened with fascination too; they had also noticed that
other candidates for the job—James Stirling, Hans Hollein—couldn't talk
about acoustics.) Gehry declaimed at length about how it was not an exact
science and that the experts all contradicted one another. This aroused
passion and strained civility. At one point, in Berlin, when Gehry managed to
arrange a supper with two of the most distinguished experts in the field, it
began harmoniously but ended in discord, so deep and wide is divergence of

opinion in this area. Failing to find the answer among wise men, he turned to empiricism. At around that time, I arrived at Gehry's office one day to find a large model of the Disney Hall's auditorium, into which nitrogen was being pumped from a cylinder on a truck parked outside. Nitrogen is a single molecule and therefore the least obstructive to sound waves, thus allowing for the purest sound. The model was as big as could reasonably be built, and would help Gehry to design the building through a process involving trial and error with sound and shape. Seeing it, one grasped the extent to which the programme culminates in sound and is therefore built around that goal; that, unlike Berlin (or Bilbao), the invisible rather than the visible is at the core of Disney Concert Hall, the body in time rather than space—ie as duration rather than tangibility. In the final model of the Disney Concert Hall, the auditorium is filled with rows of model humans, a full house sitting listening to a frozen model orchestra (figs 20, 21), mutely illustrating the programme, which seeks, like the nitrogen pump, to provide an unobstructed relationship to sound.

The audience and performers are contained within four concave walls countered by oppositionally curving dividers that echo (and exaggerate) the exterior of the building's core as they separate the seats at the sides of the orchestra from those in front of and behind it. Were one sitting in it, one would have little difficulty in seeing that the auditorium's shape is a gentle, contrapuntal, but logical response to the complex asymmetry of what one saw on the way in. Were one sitting in it and listening to music, and one's mind were to stray, briefly and only half-consciously, to one's physical context, such a recollection of the relationship of the interior to the exterior might be seen to be paralleled by, on the one hand, that between the symmetry common to the hall and the bodies that sit in it, and, on the other, the access to complexity and excitement that follows from animating that symmetry through architecture or music. The symmetry and curvature of the hall allow it to become an almost continuous surface that complements the continuity of the body, facilitating, through what it shares with it, access to the extreme articulation of singularities that, differently, music and architecture are. The interior of the auditorium leads back to the asymmetry and animation of the exterior as it leads forwards to the asymmetry and animation of the music. This ties together the orientation to the musical event performed by the building's exterior, and the event itself, in a way that allows the latter to replace the former without being detached from it. It is significant that it does this by making the architecture at the point of performance simple and symmetrical, although with a maximal subtlety, relating the auditorium's interior as much to the idea, image, or demands of the seated figure lost in her own response as to those of site or score. The Disney Concert Hall is designed for the performance and reception (presentation) of music, with each individual member of the audience as the client.

Fig. 20 (top) Frank Gehry & Associates: Walt Disney Concert Hall, Los Angeles, 1987–2003, design process model. Photo: Joshua White, 1993 © FOG&A

Fig. 21 Frank Gehry & Associates: Walt Disney Concert Hall, Los Angeles, 1987–2003, design process model. Photo: Joshua White, 1993 © FOG&A

However, these were not the clients who commissioned it. Once commissioned, it seemed at times as though everyone, including God, was trying to stop it being built. Situated on a hill in downtown Los Angeles, between Grand and Hope Streets on the west and east, and First and Second Streets on the north and south, the Concert Hall might be described as mobility on a slab, a complex array of movements rising from and within a rectangular base. Its completion will bring to a successful conclusion a work of exceptionally protracted evolution that has included not only clients changing their minds, causing significant alterations in the programme, but cost overruns in the planning stage that had nothing to do with Gehry, along with political opposition, and one of the city's biggest earthquakes.

The final design bears no sign of the project's travails, which, although depressing and worse when they occurred, may have turned out for the best inasmuch as the delays and cancellations and subsequent reconsiderations and revisions allowed it to absorb the distilled lessons of concurrent projects. Once clad with stone, now made out of metal, its early versions were contemporaneous with the Museum Island project, the final one with the Bilbao Guggenheim. Throughout, however, the elements Gehry employed arose from, or were applied to, thinking about the performance of music and the experience and needs of Los Angeles. And because it is devoted to music and built in the city Gehry knows best, it may provide an exceptional insight into his work.

Though Los Angeles is not a city in the traditional sense of an urban accumulation expanding from, but lived through, a central core, there are in it a significant number of important (ie, rich and powerful) people who think it should be. Like the Museum of Contemporary Art (MoCA), which is close by on Grand Street, the Disney Concert Hall is part of a project aimed at revitalising Los Angeles' downtown area—or giving it a downtown it never had. Gehry, in contrast, agrees with those who argue that Los Angeles has already formed itself and is linear rather than centred. Had he been asked, he would have done things differently. 'If one were logical', Gehry says, 'one would put the Disney Music Hall near the Wadsworth Auditorium. And one would have put the [new] Cathedral near McArthur Park' (in a heavily Catholic, because Hispanic, neighbourhood) 'and MoCA near LACMA' (the Los Angeles County Museum of Art, which is situated halfway between the west side and downtown, ie, half-way between where the museum audience is most heavily concentrated and the city's administrative centre).

All of Gehry's hypothetical relocations are to sites on Wilshire Boulevard, envisaging Los Angeles developed on the basis of what it actually is: a chain of distinct entities stretching from one end of the boulevard to the other. In Gehry's mind, these could all be developed so as both to interact and to be more clearly focused in regard to the locality and its needs. Mid-Wilshire, where the County Museum is and to where Gehry would move MoCA as well, would have an internal light bus service—as does, for example, Santa Monica at the seaside end of Wilshire—while there is already a subway running between there and downtown that could and should be extended to the sea. The important thing to note here is that, as ever, Gehry seeks in principle to make the most of what's already there. He has said to me more than once that 'We fought a war for democracy, but no one will really think about what we're supposed to do with it'. His is an architect's view of the political, democratic most of all in that it seeks to imagine a programme that would work for everyone practically rather than subjunctively: not what could or should work for what everyone could or should be, but what can be done with what there is, given where and what people are.

However, Gehry didn't have anything to do with the choice of the Disney Music Hall's site. Los Angeles is to have a downtown. Always a zone of absence in the evenings and at the weekends, like Wall Street in New York or Threadneedle Street and its environs in London, Los Angeles' administrative and financial district is to be enlivened by the importation of culture. In principle it should work. Everybody has a car; it should be easy to park. In practice, apart from eating a bit of Asian food, there isn't much to do in this area before or after one has ingested the culture for which one came, and it's quite a long way from where most people live.

Specifically, it's quite a long way on a very crowded freeway from where most of the people who go to art museums or concert halls live, which is the west side, in Beverley Hills or Brentwood or Westwood or Santa Monica. Were one to ask whether the original destruction of middle-class homes during the heroic period in the 1940s when Los Angeles was reinvented as a place of very cheap and plentiful water and all that can follow from that, in order to build what is now in need of enlivening, was such a good idea after all, one would need to take into account that it was performed by the Chandler family, which owns the *Los Angeles Times* and a very large part of downtown. In this respect, the Chandler Pavilion and other cultural institutions added to downtown could be seen as ways of seeking to improve the value of the Chandler family's property.

One understands that although preferring the market to the social, capitalism will employ the social when there is a market opportunity in it. There will be an enlivened downtown, where historically there was only ever a zone internationally known from *noir* movies because they were cheaply made at night using equipment that other crews needed during the day, and downtown around the courthouse and the *Los Angeles Times* building was always a good place to find an almost deserted locale in which to shoot.

It might work, because although people complain about the drive, there is an audience for music in Los Angeles and unlike museums, concert halls are not places to which people go by chance during the day. (Or don't. Marooned in a business district, MoCA is generally far less populated than LACMA except for evening openings, although this is also a reflection of its curatorial policies.) Schoenberg, Stravinsky, and on the critical side of things, Adorno, found shelter from Fascism in Los Angeles, and it has continued to be a place where the supply of, and demand for, interesting music is high.

Gehry has had plenty of experience building performance spaces—the Concord Pavilion for example—including reworking the Hollywood Bowl (1970–82) in Los Angeles itself, where he significantly improved the acoustics. He has also undertaken work for Disney. So it made sense that he should, towards the end of the last decade, have been asked to build a concert hall in downtown Los Angeles to be named after the man who brought us *Fantasia*. A site having been selected, Mrs Disney, the maximum leader's widow, handed over a down-payment, and other members of the family tossed in a bit more, to the collective tune of about 70 million dollars, to get the building built.

Then—almost with the inevitability of a movie—some rather important things started to go wrong. It had been understood from the beginning that Gehry's office could not do the engineering drawings because he didn't have enough staff, and the architectural office hired to do them—selected by the collective client—failed to produce drawings that could be used to construct the building Gehry had designed. How such a thing could happen will be a mystery to those outside the trade; that there was a good chance that it would was apparently something everyone in the trade knew all along. In any event it did, and that, along with various other feats of mismanagement, caused 60 million dollars to disappear.

One recalls the late Everett Dirkson, the last Republican known to have a sense of humour, saying about Federal spending 'A million here, a million there, and pretty soon you're talking about real money', and something like that seems to have happened with the Concert Hall. Unfortunately, there was enough real money lost to endanger the project. In the same way that American politicians will decide that we can't afford welfare mothers, although of course we can afford to subsidise the pharmaceutical industry, so too Los Angeles, which is to say the people in it who have all the money, began to behave as though 'we' could not afford the Disney Concert Hall.

The earthquake and charges of elitism helped the controversy along, to the point where the project seemed doomed. Then the (it must be said) Republican Mayor of Los Angeles, Richard Riordan, stepped into the breach. For civic reasons that may have included a social dimension, he decided he wanted it built. Costs had gone up. It wasn't the 1980s any more. Frugality rather than deficit spending was the flavour of the month. Nonetheless, the mayor assembled a group of rich people, at the head of which he persuaded Eli Broad to serve. Broad is a real-estate dealer with a large contemporary art collection, which he graciously makes accessible to the public in a building loosely based on an original design by Gehry. Finally, that job done, the Concert Hall is now to be built. The final cost is 170 million, plus the 60 million that had gone astray early in the programme's realisation.

The Disney Concert Hall was designed for a city that Gehry describes as chaotic because of its democratic nature—the democracy, I would say, though he does not, of the (American) marketplace rather than the (European) community. In Berlin, they have a plan and think one should have one—albeit one that doesn't include changing the shape of anything. But in Los Angeles a discussion about the redevelopment of downtown held by a local radio talk show, during which the Disney Concert Hall was mentioned more than once, included considerable disagreement as to whether there should be an overall plan at all.[1] Some felt the very suggestion was at odds with the spirit of the city, that freedom of the American sort depends on not having a plan (but having a market instead). Accordingly, where in Germany Gehry's response to Berlin's image of itself foundered on a misunderstanding of, or refusal to recognise, its logic, in Los Angeles the Concert Hall project became embroiled in a collective reluctance to having an image imposed on the city, even one that is understood or recognised. This means what it always means when Americans speak out against having their lives administered from above. They can say what they like, but their distrust of government leaves property developers the only ones with plans that can be put into effect. The result is that if in Berlin one can't make the changes that should be made, in Los Angeles one can't necessarily put the building where it should be put.

It is within the constraints imposed on logic by that fact, or possibly despite them, that Gehry, in the Disney Concert Hall, has designed a building that can embody and respond to the chaos he sees as a positive force in the city's view of itself. One may say that it might not be in the right place, but the city is, after all, made of the inappropriately placed—it is the only town on earth where one can find a tyre store next to one selling carpets worth thousands of dollars. It seems quite possible that Los Angeles residents hear more music in their cars than anywhere else, which is to say, in a particular place that can be in any place whatsoever. In its final form, the Disney Concert Hall makes less overt reference to the buildings near to it than it once did, except contradictorily: it continues to depart from the grid to which they conform (including MoCA, rather surprisingly given that the reputation of its architect, Arata Isoguki (1984), owes a great deal to his having based an earlier building on Marilyn Monroe's body). In its self-sufficiency, announced by its departure from the grid, it offers a democratic alternative within a locale that it will now come to define because it is more active, and at the same time, more concentrated, than what surrounds it. In Los Angeles, the idea of democracy requires the presence of more than one type of everything—of car or food or building, for example—and Gehry's architecture may be read as both producer and product of this image of a heterogeneous city—a car city with many focuses rather than a hub, calling for an architecture of singularity and motion.

As has been said, the Concert Hall has changed its skin from stone to metal in the course of its protracted development. This change came about late in the programme, and involved completely reimagining the building's appearance. Metal has introduced a greater degree of mobility into the building than was there before, although by the time the change to metal took place, stone had already been made to take on a degree of curvature to which it is traditionally unaccustomed (figs 22–26). While the Disney Music Hall was being thought and rethought due to money and earthquakes, Gehry invented a condition of the ectoplasmic in which the mass of the building becomes complicated by its surface to the point where it seems more appropriate to describe it as movements than as volumes. One can see other applications of this in the Bilbao Guggenheim, where sculptural mass is ordered by movement intensified by reflection, but through an almost continuous surface, which is not the case in the Disney Hall. One can also see it in the windows that Gehry has designed for Der Neue Zollhof development in Dusseldorf (official opening 1999, completion expected in February 2000), which deepen, or open up, or otherwise render ambiguous, the high rise's continuous facade. Both of these will be further discussed in Chapter 4. The Disney Concert Hall uses the skin to make a looser volumetric structure than the Guggenheim's, creating changes of movement around the central hall that intensify and become elaborate on the Grand Avenue and First Street sides of the site, where it is close to the road. On the other two sides, they become slower and simpler, making a background to the separate founders' room building, constructed from a shinier metal than the hall, and a small amphitheatre on the Second Street end between the offices and the hall. The shape of the founders' room seems derived from the glass restaurant that appears in earlier versions (fig 22): its plan shows that it was developed out of a circle, which is tight and circular as it abuts the main building but frays or splays out as it faces the corner of First and Hope—loosely adjusting itself to a right angle.

This seems symptomatic both of the programme's development and of Gehry's practice taken as a whole. Metal is in Gehry's work the extension of an extension. It is not a matter of what it makes possible, since one can in theory make anything do anything, but of what it makes imaginable. Metal has allowed a greater departure from unified volume than was imaginable when the Disney Concert Hall was clad in stone, but this is a departure from a volume already ectoplasmic rather than skeletal.

One reason for this may be that metal is lighter than stone. Or perhaps it is simply that it has associations with mobility that stone does not: jumbo jets are made of light-coloured metal, for example. One of the first things one notices when comparing the final model with what Gehry describes as an 'interim stage before things went bad' (fig 23), when the cladding was still stone, is that the later one simplifies the transitions to the street on the Grand Avenue and First Street sides. Gehry has had to do less to establish an idea of levitation. The thick wall on First that supports part of the entrance's covering has gone, replaced with a simpler collapse of roof into wall, which

Fig. 22 Frank Gehry & Associates: Walt Disney Concert Hall, Los Angeles, 1987–2003, competition model. Photo: Joshua White, 1988 © FOG&A

Fig. 23 Frank Gehry & Associates: Walt Disney Concert Hall, Los Angeles, 1987–2003, design process model. Photo: Brian Yoo, 1991 © FOG&A

Fig. 24 (top) Frank Gehry & Associates: Walt Disney Concert Hall, Los Angeles, 1987–2003, design process model. Photo: Brian Yoo, 1991 © FOG&A

Fig. 25 Frank Gehry & Associates: Walt Disney Concert Hall, Los Angeles, 1987–2003, competition model. Photo: Tom Bonner, 1988 © FOG&A

Fig. 26 Frank Gehry & Associates: Walt Disney Concert Hall, Los Angeles, 1987–2003, competition model. Photo: Tom Bonner, 1988 © FOG&A

dispenses with the feeling of something being propped up, of motion suspended at the site's perimeter, and seen to be suspended, substituting a gentler movement, which folds into the site as it marks its limit (fig. 32). Similarly, the Grand Avenue side, where before there were a number of transitional movements that kept the building suspended between horizontal and vertical as it approached the street, is still extremely active but now less a matter of angles than of curving planes, which are closer to the vertical than those behind them, rather than, as previously, the reverse (fig. 31).

This returns us to a question introduced in Chapter 1. If one may say that there doesn't have to be so much explicit invocation of the anti-gravitational—by keeping surfaces off the ground or delaying their arrival at it—when Gehry uses metal rather than stone, because the metal is already less tied to gravity or stasis, then one is saying that his use of either material depends as much on its signifying potential as its structural virtues—on what it stands for as much as what it does. The Disney Concert Hall ended up being clad in metal because very late in the programme's chequered life the clients decided that they didn't like stone because they had seen what had happened in the American Centre, where the money had run out before the stone was properly protected and the building had therefore become discoloured. At the same time, they had also become aware of the Bilbao Guggenheim's use of titanium. At first, Gehry balked, explaining that one couldn't just recoat the building. Then the office building and some other components were introduced or reintroduced, and 'So one day we had a burst of energy: What if we did it in metal? We started to correct things. It became a new project'. The design had to be reconsidered because they were now working with a material that stands for lightness as stone does not. The building was now less about things (planes) held up by other things. Already light, metal doesn't require as elaborate a rhetoric of the antigravitational as stone. This has implications for the experience and interpretation of Gehry's architecture that it is now time to discuss in greater detail.

Early in the programme, there was going to be a hotel on the site (fig 24) to whose continuity with the verticality of the adjacent buildings the hall would have opposed an activated horizontality. The hall is made out of curving movements where the hotel contains none, has a mostly blank facade where the hotel's is filled with rows of windows, and contrasts to that measured use of glass a concentration of it at the end of the building away from the hotel, so that the entrance to the hall reads as a demonstration of all that glass is not allowed to do in the buildings around it. Fig 24 also shows how at that stage the scheme brought its environs together, connecting to the tall buildings to its south by repetition—the hotel in fig 24 is about as tall as the building on the other side of Second Street, while the hall is roughly the same height as the courthouse on the other side of First. This version envisaged the Concert Hall as a transitional zone, leading away from the tall commercial buildings to its south, crowded at the hotel end, but at the other, where the entrance is, opening up into glass—glittering, continuous, transparent, at once enveloping and not opaque, wire mesh reimagined as a transparent surface, perhaps.

Another early version included a bridge to the courthouse (figs 22, 25)— a link some would find ominous. At that stage, the hotel had been replaced with offices, subsequently eliminated but since restored, while other elements once present but no longer part of the programme included a small hall for chamber music, a bookshop, a restaurant, and an area covered with a glass canopy extended from the entrance, which was to be for outdoor activities (figs 25–29).

The canopy recalls the Pergamon addition in the Berlin project, and in general these early versions suggest other comparisons with Museum Island. The manner in which one moves around the building and the way the complex runs along Grand Avenue in the model shown in fig 24, for example, recall the combination of restaurant, galleries and bridge that joined the Neues to the Altes along the Kupfergraben, as, less straightforwardly, does the final version. There is another similarity with Museum Island that may be less obvious. Just as Gehry used curvature and buildings tilted towards or away from the street to activate and unify the Berlin site, all the models for the Disney Hall show it to have been tilted

Fig. 27   Frank Gehry & Associates: Walt Disney Concert Hall, Los Angeles, 1987–2003, competition model. Photo: Tom Bonner, 1988 © FOG&A

Fig. 28   Frank Gehry & Associates: Walt Disney Concert Hall, Los Angeles, 1987–2003, competition model. Photo: Tom Bonner, 1988 Copyright FOG&A

Fig. 29 Frank Gehry & Associates: Walt Disney Concert Hall, Los Angeles, 1987–2003, competition model. Photo: Tom Bonner, 1988 © FOG&A

onto the site—orientated to or derived from an entrance that was always intended to be at the corner of First Street and Grand Avenue. In Berlin it had been a question of reworking a group of buildings arranged (unworkably) on a grid but otherwise with much to disunify them; in Los Angeles it is a question of animating a section of a grid. By getting shapes to twist around it, making use of the corner and allowing for plenty of varied movement around the Hall, Gehry makes it specific to its downtown location—between office buildings and the courthouse—by undermining the rectangle it occupies.

It undermines it, however, only in order to reiterate it as an idea that has become layered and reworked. Similarly, the Disney Hall's exterior departs in all directions from the building's core but ultimately repeats it: what Gehry does to the rectilinearity of the site is directly comparable to the way in which he treats the main volume present on it. The rectangle is reorientated to the entrance at its north-east corner, the general drift towards the north-east being countered by the founders' room on the north-western side, while at the other end, the offices run the length of the block (fig 30). The founders' room is shinier and a more concentrated assemblage of movements than the hall itself, and could also be seen to complete the movement that begins on Grand Avenue and is continued around the corner

Fig. 30 Frank Gehry & Associates: Walt Disney Concert Hall, Los Angeles, 1987–2003, final design model. Photo: Whit Preston, 1999 © FOG&A

onto First Street but ends just past the entrance, when the curving metal, which has until now run along the street, is pulled back into the site. The founders' room could therefore be said to read as the end of a sequence, at which point complex and rapid movements give way to slower, simpler ones when approached from Grand Avenue (figs 31–33). When seen from the other side, however, it acts as an introductory contrast to those larger movements of form, marking the location of the entrance (concealed from that position), by drawing attention to itself and thereby to that end of the building. The whole vista is set well back from the street when seen from Hope while spilling onto it along Grand—the two possibilities coming together along First. In introducing asymmetry into the site, Gehry brings the building to the street from which one accesses it while setting it back from the other, so that one is onto the site very quickly with plenty of space outside the building in which to wander around once one is there. This adds to one's impression that the Concert Hall is self-contained while at the same time open to the outside. The basic condition of the automobile driver is to be lost in the music on the radio but engaged with an outside entirely made of movement. (Everyone at the concert will have driven there.)

The building is made out of two cubes, tilted into one another so as to make a shallow 'v'. Forms have accumulated around these, which together

Fig. 31 Frank Gehry & Associates: Walt Disney Concert Hall, Los Angeles, 1987–2003, final design model. Photo: Whit Preston, 1998 © FOG&A

Fig. 32 Frank Gehry & Associates: Walt Disney Concert Hall, Los Angeles, 1987–2003, final design model. Photo: Whit Preston, 1998 © FOG&A

Fig. 33 Frank Gehry & Associates: Walt Disney Concert Hall, Los Angeles, 1987–2003, final design model. Photo: Whit Preston, 1998 © FOG&A

with the skin that joins them, restate and extend the basic structure as vistas when one is at a distance. When one is nearby, they are close encounters with particular concentrations of surface as subdivided volume, or volume intersected by planes, complicated in either case by movement through and across it. The metal cladding describes a movement like a skirt's—integral to because separable from the body it presents, reorders, and conceals—folding and turning and stopping and starting as it stretches out from the rectangular core to join it to the street and to enfold the auditorium's ancillary functions and details (fig 34).

Gehry starts with volume—in the Disney Concert Hall, one to be filled with sound—but has become more and more engaged in using surface to complicate mass. How planes function in his work in relation to volume will be further discussed in Chapter 4. But to do that, and especially in terms of the Disney Concert Hall, it seems necessary further to consider surface as movement rather than plane in Gehry's architecture, which is to say, as mobility and continuity rather than facet and aspect. Skirts are joined to the body only at the waist or hips, otherwise being free to move in relation to what they cover and thus re-present.

Talk of skirts implicates Gehry's use of the idea of the ectoplasmic in an argument started by Gottfried Semper (1803–79). This is a dispute about what

Fig. 34 Frank Gehry & Associates: Walt Disney Concert Hall, Los Angeles,1987–2003, final design model. Photo: Whit Preston, 1998 © FOG&A

buildings should be like, partly in respect to what architecture may be said to be in a genealogical sense, and partly in respect to what it has to be in order to be good for you. This takes the form of an argument to the effect that solidity in architecture is destined to give way to a representation of a less inert surface: 'even where the erection of firm masonry is required, it forms only the inner and hidden scaffolding, stowed behind the true and legitimate representation of the wall, the decorated fabric'.[2] Not surprisingly, the question of surface developed to the point where it threatens to do something to form other than maintain it, implicates one in the attendant problem of ornament, wherein one finds an odd but familiar golden rule: when surface does more than ornament (an idea of) form it is said to have become ornamental. Semper seems relevant to Gehry because he appears to have most thoroughly thought through the idea of architecture as always a composite sign; the thing and its ornamentation as an interaction that is the event.

Michael Podro, from whose text the Semper quotation is taken, also quotes him when insisting that 'Clothes… both bring out and correct the forms of the body: "They clothe the naked form with an elucidating symbolism"'.[3] Of this, Podro goes on to say that the 'notion of realisation, of bringing out aspects of the body or material or construction, of imparting value to them, is a recurrent feature of Semper's thought', and I want to suggest that, in Gehry's work, materials comparably elucidate form by attaching it to their own connotations. They don't supplement the form so much as they *trans*form it. The form is only conceivable as that which awaits supplementation; it is not complete until it has been supplemented. The programme's components having been assembled, it is retrospectively seen to have awaited its realisation from the outside in. It was this that required the project to be entirely rethought once the decision (or demand) had been made that it be of metal rather than stone.

A little later, Podro quotes Semper on reality: 'Every artistic production... and all enjoyment of art... presupposes a certain temper of the carnival, to express it in modern terms—the carnival half-light is the true atmosphere of art. The denial of reality is necessary where the form, as a symbol charged with significance, is to emerge as the self-contained human creation'.[4] Regarding which Podro makes a comment about the assumptions underlying Semper's attachment of connotations to forms that fits Gehry's work like a glove: 'Semper's sense of the... play between the real and what is suggested, would in eighteenth-century terms already have been called 'artistic appearance'; the modern expression would perhaps be interpretative seeing, looking for a feature or aspect of an object in such a way that implies that flexibility of the viewer's mind'.[5]

There are several points or images here with which one may associate Gehry: the subversion of the real by signification; the human as self-contained and creative; the viewer with a democratic mind. Semper's versions of these are not popular topics in contemporary writing about architecture. Karsten Harries seems to find Semper a threat to Heideggerian authenticity, while Mark Wigley sees him as a source of modernist self-contradiction.[6] At the same time, Harries' book despairs of architecture and mentions Gehry once, in connection with Derrida and the difficulty of philosophical engagement with the architectural and vice versa;[7] Wigley's disapproves of it and doesn't mention him at all. Semper's critical fortune may explain Gehry's.

Harries employs Michael Fried's distinction between art and theatricality to ask 'Can we still today idealise authenticity?'[8] He proceeds from there to say that we can, but that to do so would require that a collective experience offered by the theatre, but in fact precluded by a theatricality for which Semper was in large part responsible, would have to be reclaimed. He uses Semper to rehearse Nietzsche's infatuation and then disgust with Wagner, for whom Semper built a theatre.[9] Harries' argument is very subtle and I cannot do it justice here. Elsewhere, for example, he talks of Semper's insistence that the heart of architecture is the hearth.[10] But he sees Semper's idea of cladding's aesthetic function as setting the terms for an ultimately fatal disconnection between authentic purpose and aesthetic appearance, and it is in the early stages of his discussion of that wrong turn that he first introduces him to us. Discussing ornament and Adolph Loos' relationship to it (it is also through Loos that we come to Semper in Wigley's book), Harries says that 'Loos' attack on ornament is... quite compatible with his recognition of the fundamental importance of cladding, which, as suggested by Gottfried Semper's paradigm to which Loos is so evidently indebted... may also have an aesthetic function'. Harries quotes Semper:

> The reasons for cladding things are numerous. At times it is a protection against bad weather—oil base paint, for example, on wood, iron, or stone; at times there are hygienic reasons for it—as in the case of enamelled tiles that cover the wall surfaces in the bathroom; at times it is the means to a specific effect—as in the colour painting of statues, the tapestries on walls, the veneer on wood.[11]

To which he adds, dryly:

> The order is telling: first the weather, then hygiene, and finally features intended to put us in a certain mood. If what is to be built is a prison, the architect may want to arouse fear and horror; if a church, a sense of reverence; if an inn, a sense of gaiety; if a house, a homey feeling... But all this does not make him an artist.[12]

He immediately follows up this assertion with a (rhetorical) question: 'Could "cladding for the sake of aesthetic effect" not serve as a definition of ornament?'[13] Clearly it could, and equally clearly, metal cladding, elucidating a form it has redrawn, obviates what Harries describes as Loos' 'law of cladding': that 'we must work in such a way that a confusion of the material clad with its cladding is impossible'.[14] Leaving aside for the moment the desire codified by that law, it is significant that while Gehry's use of metal couldn't perform that confusion, it performs one like it—which, technologically and retrospectively speaking, could be said to be implicit in it—in that what are clad are surfaces that confuse (elucidate anew) the core's relationship to the exterior through intensification and extension, not least by eroding or qualifying the idea of the skeletal and replacing it with that of the exoskeletal. It is here that Wigley's use of Semper becomes relevant to a discussion of Gehry.

Wigley wrestles with the question of whether modernism is good for you; the match is a draw. Making extensive use of Semper and Loos, he proves conclusively that Le Corbusier especially, and modernist architects generally, were disingenuous about the question of fashion, but fails to show that this did any harm to the architecture. His study of the relationship between the ideas of clothing (where, again, hygiene is seen to play a depressingly prominent role in the discussion) and architecture, if, as is now usual in architectural criticism, almost thrilling in its casual prudishness, is compelling and wholly persuasive. It traces the idea of cladding from its origin in Semper to its logical self-extinction in its close reading by Hendrik Berlage, who 'expressed reservations about Semper's emphasis on the surface mask and attempted to ... effac[e] Semper's distinction between the structural prop and the fabric surface'.[15] Then he describes a Berlage that anticipates Gehry: 'The surface assumes a visible thickness but creates an impression of thinness inasmuch as that thickness is understood to be structural. The self-supporting surface rises up, like some kind of magic carpet, to define the space'.[16]

The issue, perhaps, is that of the self-supporting surface, which, by definition, is not the surface in the sense of a facet of a volume, but is rather, by the same definition, independent of volume because it is self-supporting (or seems to be). This is the magic that, for Harries, subverts structure's primacy over surface—deferring core into covering, essence into appearance. For Wigley, it is the origin of modernist disingenuousness.

Gehry has said of the nineteenth-century taste for ornament that 'while it didn't make sense to keep doing that, it does make sense to have something in the building that is interesting to the human'. The idea of ornamentation implies a whole that has been supplemented. But in Gehry's work, the idea of ornament has been displaced into the skin itself, into which the ectoplasmic emphasis of the building also displaces, from the inside to the outside, the idea of structure.

It is possible to see architecture's history from the nineteenth century until now as one in which ornament gave way to transparency, which in its turn gave way to blankness. First there was a skin that embellishes but also conceals, then the elimination of concealment and the exteriorisation of the interior—the outside only an expression of and passage to the inside—and now an architecture whose exterior has another relationship to the interior: neither embellishing nor reflecting, it stands apart from what it enfolds.[17]

The ectoplasmic surface with which Gehry works should be considered in the light of the passage from transparency to opacity—ie from modernism to after modernism. The reflective surfaces of Bilbao or the Disney Concert Hall, in being light and blank, gesture towards the former while being opaque. At various times, Gehry has employed them in different combinations, transparency and opacity being the terms of earlier versions of the Disney Concert Hall and of the Museum Island project, in both of which transparency was also a kind of surface, arcing over opaque structures as a plane, or breaking them up with moments of complex volume. This interaction of transparency and opacity is fundamental to the Disney Music Hall's realisation of an architecture in which volume, mass, and structure become identified with an architecture of surface. It is an architecture of extension, and therefore of the temporal rather than the spatially specific.

And by virtue of its being viewed as extension without mass (as surface), it is an architecture of weightlessness, and therefore of convergent implications rather than reductive explication (the material's own truth is ungrounded by serving as the ground for a symbolic array). It is an architecture of space without skeleton or gravity and therefore of a subsumed idea of the destructured architectural—architecture without the grid. Gehry breaks things away from one another and then finds new ways of putting them back together. Surfaces become self-supporting through Gehry's focus on their attributes. Opaque surfaces are pulled away from what they conceal by being interesting in themselves, having a shape that clearly masks, hinting at, rather than disappearing into a reiteration of, the form it clads—which itself performs the same restatement as it joins forms together. Transparent surfaces recontextualise transparency. Similarly, Gehry defeats the grid by finding a life for the programme that may be reconciled to it but is not determined by it.

Gehry has said that it was Le Corbusier's paintings that allowed him to think himself free of the grid. Such a freedom could give rise to a number of possibilities, but they would all have to be ones that would permit a certain amount of variable time into space. The grid eliminates the temporal, subsuming near and far, centre and periphery, in a regime of absolute repetition and simultaneity, of space without time. (In this respect one might see that Heidegger's hostility to technology's abolition of time in favour of a spatialised world, a world that robbed existence of its authenticity by being there all at once and therefore not experiencable through time, is directed beyond the contemporary and technological as we know them, towards a more fundamental problem, which is something like the idea of the map as an inauthentic model, of the Cartesian grid as a misleading cartography.)

If in Gehry's work freedom from the grid has meant access to ideas or experiences of mobility that are not predicated on oppositions between the horizontal and vertical, and a greater access to the possibilities of discontinuity—of the arelational and nonrelational—than might otherwise be possible, both lead directly to Heidegger and to deorigination.

The Disney Concert Hall rearranges Heidegger's model to bring forth a potential contained in a site that may be described as a social space whose natural origins have been entirely obliterated and were in any case never continuous with what replaced them. A site, then, that from Heidegger's point of view has been ripped away from man by an uncontrollable and malevolent technology. If Gehry is Hegelian in bringing forth something from nothing, and Kantian in developing a project that works as a thing in itself, in concentrating in the Disney Concert Hall on a retrieval of the site—a re-presentation of it that gives it value by giving it meaning—he is Heideggerian: his buildings are attached to their context through being detached from it. But, as noted, his is a Heideggerianism that stands the old Nazi on his head. Gehry makes buildings that call for Heideggerian readings, not despite, but because, he is so comfortable in the world Heidegger loathed. His architecture uses the idea of the grounded within the context of the ungrounded field of contemporary techno-capitalism, which it understands to have replaced the ground so necessary to Heidegger's authentic being. It is in this a Heideggerianism that has dispensed with Heideggerian authenticity, the unavailability of which as a credible idea to Gehry is echoed in his rejection of the cult of truth to materials.

This freedom from a naturalism that is at once a productivism, the hermeneutic passing always in Heidegger from labour to being—the one found in the other through the latter providing the critical terms for the former's (re)discovery of itself as the realisation of its own ground—leads in turn to the other Heidegger whose thinking Gehry's practice invokes: the late twentieth-century one provided by Derrida. Gehry's has much in common with Derrida's thinking (though little of this came to light during that mad moment in the Reagan years when some American architects actually thought they could get something going by trying to involve Derrida in architecture). Derrida, the philosopher of non-origination, developed Heidegger to the point of theorising the infinite deferral of being as a condition only ever present as representation: iteration as reiteration and reverberation. This has allowed Derrida to see texts as convergences of other (precedent but also conceivably simultaneous) texts with a subtlety—ie, an ability to describe the extent to which they are interwoven yet remain disconnected—denied to others. A similar range of interpenetrations and discontinuities is to be found in Gehry's works, which should be described as reconventions of the deoriginated. In drawing, and therefore in architecture or any structure, the ungrounded is that which is free of the grid—which could well be a freedom produced by a layering or other simultaneity of grids in which no overall co-ordinates could be discerned, as, in Derrida, texts destabilise other texts while all being textual. Or it could be a freedom that comes from ignoring—just as it has been said that Francis Bacon was able to have a successful career by ignoring Marcel Duchamp's existence.[18] In Le Corbusier, Gehry saw that one could only get things to destabilise one another by emphasising their mutual differences rather than being indifferent to something about them—for example, by not caring about what was most important *to* them.

It is possible that what one gets when one does without the grid is the fold, mention of which suggests the book of that title about Leibnitz and the Baroque by Deleuze, philosopher of the surface without depth.[19] Folding means moving in and out without discontinuity or rupture. Gehry sees the fold as providing a space or receptacle, comparable to the fold in the mother's garment where she holds her baby. But in Gehry's architecture, the surface tends to move in and out, not to provide a resting place, but to complicate—add layers of richness to—movement, around the building and in and out of it.

Accordingly, in earlier versions of the Disney Concert Hall (and before that in the Vitra Design Museum, as well as most recently in the Bilbao Guggenheim), cladding attributes its ectoplasmic quality to the building as a whole: transparency that collapses the outside into the inside, and vice versa, and opacity through which the outside may pretend to offer no clue to what it describes and implies. The self-supporting becomes less about supporting than about activating. One may say that in the earlier versions of the Disney Concert Hall, Gehry used stone and glass to replace the material surface with a spatiality that was not of it but was added to it by what it was made to do. But in the later, metal, version he does something much closer to what he did earlier in his career with wire mesh. He uses metal and glass to activate the design through what the material surface can do in itself, cladding the building in a skin that drives the design rather than being brought to life by it. Both involved a self-supporting exterior, but the later version takes the idea further. One way of thinking about the difference is that the opaque surfaces are now closer to the properties of glass than ever before, and Gehry has always presented glass as contradiction: reflective (ie, not transparent) and transparent; a surface that throws light back and that one may look into.

In this regard, the Guggenheim Bilbao could be seen to have a precedent in Gehry's use of transparency as an articulated surface in the Nationale Nederlanden building in Prague (fig 35), (where one may also see the tentative origins of the Dusseldorf windows, which articulate the blank surface and make it spatially ambiguous by bombarding the plane of the wall with other planes). In Gehry's work, transparency's articulation as a surface blurs the passage from outside to inside, causing a confusion that subverts the free passage proffered by glass, here enhanced by the building's departure from the simple vertical. Transparency becomes a ground for a complicated distancing of inside from outside, allowing the building to reach out beyond the space it occupies, to gather light from outside, and, most importantly, to allow its own form to be a matter of a shimmering surface of interpenetration as both perception and idea. This is the transparent ectoplasmic, where, however, transparency does not cause the surface to disappear, or the inside to become the outside, but is instead used to open up the gap between the two ideas. The Dusseldorf windows literalise that gap by extending the window into the exterior, at the same time pulling the interior out of its grid by introducing into it another presence. The self-supporting surface, having come to substitute the idea of movement for that of support, is then free to expand the surface into a more elaborate zone of planar convergences.

Perhaps the relationship between Gehry's use of surface and Berlage's wall as described by Wigley could be put historically. It returns one to Gehry's view that it is no longer sensible to talk about truth to materials. It meant something for the wall to be really self-supporting when Berlage did

Fig. 35 Frank Gehry & Associates: Nationale-Nederlanden Building, Prague, 1992–1996, Photo: Mark Salette, 1997 Copyright FOG&A

it. He worked with brick as well as with metal, at a time when one could imagine buildings that couldn't be built. Now, though, when anything that can be drawn can be built, the pressure to make the building do more than realise the drawing is proportionally increased. For Gehry, it seems to be the defining issue. That a wall is self-supporting can no longer be exciting in itself—it is, thanks to contemporary technology, not an engineering feat but an architectural choice. Hence the need to exceed it as an engineering fact. The issues raised by it are all Semper's, however, in that what is at stake continues to be a question of what can be associated with the wall as a self-supporting surface. Gehry has turned this into a question of how to make materials connote movement.

This in its turn destabilises one's idea of drawing, which is to say, of where one is to find the idea of the building. Gehry describes the way he works as being just like the way he draws: 'Build up, back to the beginning, over and over again. Process adds layers of richness'. A way of working by adding but then starting again, then, whose goal is a richness that must be more than a record or confirmation of the process that produced it. There should be layers of it, as the process that produced it was layered, but these layers should be of movements only possessed (connoted) by the building once it has been built. To work as Gehry does—in the case of the Disney Concert Hall, more than he might have liked—by building up while returning to the beginning, suggests discovery as rediscovery: reiteration that is not repetition. Discovery as rediscovery is at least formally genealogical; something is teleologically related to its starting point. Matisse said that a painting should be as good as the first sketch made on a restaurant napkin. Gehry's response to that anecdote was 'I'd even say it should be better than the first sketch'. To which he immediately added, 'I would even say it's got to be as good as the thing you first had in your head'. Adding layers of richness brings with it the idea of ornament as addition—implicitly, of something with beginnings other than those with which one began—which is also the product of reconsideration, a reframing of the original by what finishes it.

But what he reframes it with is that which can't be drawn. Gehry has reversed modernist transparency, itself the product of the elimination of ornament, most obviously by enlisting glass in delaying the passage from the inside to the outside rather than making it a matter of immediacy. He uses glass to open buildings to the outside, but in doing so does not suggest an uninterrupted passage from within to without. His use of glass finds meaning not in clarity but in complicating that which proposes it, and is in that respect the opposite of, say, what glass does in Mies van der Rohe's National Gallery in Berlin (1962–1968). In a manner continuous with his use of glass and the idea of transparency, Gehry has returned the building's facade to the status of a skin that conceals the inside, where modernism had sought to eliminate the skin as far as possible in the interests of an aesthetic of revealing that was certainly not entirely unconnected to an ethic of revelation. Adolf Loos' declaration that ornament was criminal was surely fuelled by the notion that truth lay on the inside, from which it would be but a small step to making the exterior express rather than conceal an interior because concealment was bad and therefore revealing was good.

Much of Wigley's argument is taken up with demonstrating, convincingly, that modernism really used white to cover things up while talking about stripping them bare. The problem is seen by Wigley to originate in Semper's argument that the Greeks only used white marble as a ground to paint on, leading to a theory of architecture in which: 'The sense of the naked is only produced within the supplementary layer itself. The body of the building never becomes visible, even where it coincides with the decorative layer'.[21] But one could argue that the uncovered is only of interest when it is a representational rather than presentational concept—ie when opposed to covering. In itself, the uncovered is inarticulate: as I've discussed elsewhere,[22] it is only when bodies are clothed that one can make judgements about this person's decision to wear that, which are also the terms within which the body communicates through being partially or completely unclothed. That is the sense in which nakedness is a cultural gesture, an extreme sartorial option. *Genesis* is a story about God becoming cross when language is invented. Wigley's irritation with Le Corbusier is understandable as an extension of that tradition. As a protest against the inseparability of the body from clothing, it recalls a truth about modernism implied in the distinction that TJ Clark makes between the nude and the naked in discussing Manet's *Olympia*.[23] The nude is unavailable to modernism because it is not the culmination of uncovering, which is the essence of nakedness, where something has been stripped away; the modern is predicated on the loss of innocence. Wigley is clear about this, but it is a clarity that flirts with circularity. His criticism of Le Corbusier is not directed at what might have been asserted were anything left uncovered, but at a disingenuous use of the gesture—or language—of uncovering. It was criticality that was betrayed, not what—the truth of any materials for example—was obscured. Had it not been obscured, it would have been its lack of covering that Wigley would have seen as significant rather than its presence as a combination of—for example, material—properties: they would have been there only to represent the concept of uncovering as truth. In contradisctinction to the values put forth by Wigley, Gehry's reversal of modernist transparency follows Semper, and is in this indifferent—an indifference that is Heideggerian in a counter-Heideggerian way—to the idea of uncovering. In Gehry, as in Semper, cutting across, or in place of, the pathos of a theory of modernism that grounds it in criticality, is the assertion that the human finds itself in ornament, its absence only signifying another kind of ornament or mode of presentation: the partially or wholly uncovered. Both are in practice—so much for truths—unavailable to architecture because buildings are structures rather than beings. Otherwise, to build something that was partially or entirely uncovered would be either to fail to build something or to defer functions into others.

However, as Wigley shows too, modernist architects used white to propose continuity as well as absence. Modernism used it to cover up the discontinuity it rediscovered or relocated elsewhere and in its own terms, but in so doing it also approximated architecture to drawing, which is whiteness articulated by lines that mark the edges of surfaces or the limits of volumes. Gehry works with surfaces that exceed drawing, and not only because they are seldom flat.

This raises a question about Gehry's relationship to the contemporary world, filled with blank white surfaces that, because they are electronic screens, are alive before anything is put on them. The meaning or conventional associations of whiteness have changed since the early twentieth century, once signifying absence awaiting activation, now active. (Where we used to write on paper, we now interact with the screen.) This change is in my opinion apparent in Gehry's interest in colour and transparency, to which I am relating his use of reflectivity.

All of these cannot be drawn, and one gathers that with Gehry, they precede the drawing rather than being added to it, reversing the terms of the ornamental, and adding to the connotations of the idea of the self-supporting in his work. Of the Disney Concert Hall one would also say that the model filled with nitrogen was also engaged with that which was essential to the programme but could not be drawn. Colour is a presiding interest for him, carried furthest in schemes like the rejected proposal for the roof of the Experience Music Project—where the client could handle Jimi Hendrix but not Frank Gehry. Colour is the ultimate expression of the self-supporting, irreducible to its medium (one can have the same red in watercolour or oil paint) and always characterising forms to which it is applied, robbing their shape of final authority. Semper was an avid champion of polychrome. Heidegger, on the other hand, imagined the Greek temple to present one with an undisturbed vista of unprotected stone. Colour was, for him, pure phenomena, hermeneutically silent because in itself it conceals nothing, and is therefore not the place where being may be (as ever, partially) revealed. But to conceal nothing is to let it be present, and colour is a force, and as such only nothing to the extent that it is not a thing. As nothing but a force, colour is the appearance of the self-supporting that erodes the priority of what actually supports it (and with it the priority of the actual). Gehry wants to make buildings out of it, and if colour as nothing but a force were to be a starting point for architecture, it need make no difference whether the colour was that of the material itself, for example stone or metal, or applied to it.

Colour, though, is less of a concern in the Disney Concert Hall, or in Bilbao, than brightness. With metal, Gehry has a material that gathers light to it as glass does, but differently, sending more of it back. In the Disney Concert Hall, the metal is used in the context of an arrangement of forms containing as many discontinuities as continuities, unlike in the Bilbao Guggenheim, where continuity is qualified in a different way, by movement as planes that constantly redirect a slower, massive but equally weightless, group of volumetric movements. The idea of continuity is established by the metal, and maintained by the use of curves and folds and wrapping around corners. (The material's innate condition becomes its rhetorical condition, truth retained for its practical usefulness to illusion.) While appealing to an idea of surface and thus of continuity, his buildings are also, in effect, bodies made of discontinuity, ie, of singularities rather than repetitions. In the case of the Disney Concert Hall—first conceived in stone and then in metal, but always made of planes that were wavier where they met the street than at the core—Gehry's use of discontinuity relates directly to music and its performance and reception.

As I shall say about the Bilbao Guggenheim and looking, the exterior of the Disney Concert Hall sets one up for listening. Seen as one approaches, the entrance to the Hall is made of curving, horizontally orientated movements surrounding and leading to angular, vertically orientated ones, all describing forms that are not repeated elsewhere. The passage from outside to inside is from two kinds of speed and movement—where degrees of curvature qualify speed, and angles and breaks make the movement stop and start again somewhere nearby, or overlap one another—to a symmetrical, gently curving interior that has to do with the implied rather than explicit movement made available by stillness, with sitting rather than walking, listening rather than looking.

The Disney Concert Hall sets a specifically Los Angles audience up for listening, by which I mean that is presents the idea of music in terms and a context recognisable to the locals, at two immediately discernible levels that have to do with the idea of the individual listener. In this respect, it invites discussion in terms of what Deleuze and Guattari call 'psychosocial types' and, complementarily, of what they describe as accompanying but irredudicible to them.

For example, as noted, the building erupts off the top of a slab that could in theory support anything. This is in keeping with the Californian symbolism of provisionality and the fresh start: it makes a space for itself by positing one from which it can disassociate itself. The office and parking-lot structure now contains a performance area and other facilities for the California Institute of the Arts, so that part of the stone-clad building at the Second Street end is populated by those aspiring to perform in the silver hall, but otherwise, visually, there is interpenetration but not continuity between the stone and the metal parts of the complex, while continuity but not repetition unites the metal-clad elements. Interpenetration but not continuity is the condition experienced by the driver of the car, listening to music in a private space while moving through a public one at speed (while continuity as a condition within which singularities occur could be a description of music, and does describe time and how events happen in it). One may add that freeway traffic is about convergences and gentle curves but not, like movement on the grid of what Californians call 'surface streets', stops and starts and right angles. Speed and movement in Gehry's buildings work similarly. His architecture has long been made of intersections between movements that do not stop moving, rather than progressing through starts and stops according to the dictates of a grid. Curves lead to right angles on the outside of the building, faster movement giving way to slower when, once under the canopy, one sees actual verticals and horizontals. The passage described by the metal on the exterior culminates in the interior's reconciliation of curvature with the rectilinear—which serves quite a different purpose from the visual detail on the outside, being meant to facilitate the transference of one's engagement from the visual to the auditory. One notes that the interiors of cars are also made of gentle curves, the driver comfortable but orientated. It may be coincidental or it may have to do with the sensitivity of car designers to the demands of acoustics, but the average southern Californian should feel comfortable in the Disney Hall's auditorium, in the sense that there should be something reassuringly familiar about it. It distantly recalls the spaces one usually sits in when engaged with movement and listening to music.

Likewise, the Disney Concert Hall articulates, in its eruption and dissimilarity from its neighbours, the democratic chaos Gehry loves. But in his practice, this chaos becomes channelled, retaining chaotic energy through an ordering that involves sustained disordering, beginning with the disordering of the grid, which customises the site to the programme. Movements are not accompanied by counter-movements so much as by other movements, or by counter-movements that are not symmetrical in their complementarity. (For example, the relationship between the left and right of the entrance, seen from the front (fig 32): on the left of the steps is an articulated volume that incorporates a number of movements and elements that lead into it but which, were it unaffected by those, could be read as the inverted negative complement of the positive form across the steps from it.) Gehry's is a sustained aesthetic of the singular within the flow, and when correspondences occur (on the exterior, not in the auditorium) they are never exact. The democratic is chaotic in that its investment in singularity precludes order based on repetition—it implicitly valorises heterogeneity.

To describe the Disney Concert Hall in this way, as reflecting or expressive of some fundamental elements of the structure out of which subjectivity constructs itself in response to Los Angeles, is to say that Gehry's buildings look at home in Los Angeles for reasons that include, but also go beyond, their being embodiments of an aesthetic conceived in no small measure by way of the earthquake codes and other local conditions. But there is a sense in which the reason they look at home in Los Angeles is not because they are specifically about or peculiar to it, but because they are peculiar to the specifically contemporary, whose realisation Los Angeles is—for better or worse. Los Angeles is a city made of structures that can look like anything capable of being built; in which citizens go from place to place in spaces filled with music (sound chambers with wheels). It is a city, therefore, that is not a city because it is made out of the mobility and privacy of the car rather than the ambulatory pace and communal space of the pedestrian, eliminating the idea of the communal except provisionally, as space shared on the road or specific to a function (for example a musical performance). It is post-urban in the sense that it is a suburbanism committed for that reason to 'remember' the urban, which can, however, thanks to the mobility of the car and the decentredness consequent on its being a confederacy of suburbs without an 'urb', be anywhere. It is city in which the symbolic has triumphed always and already in advance—its sunny constancy a *tabula rasa* for simulation. There are, for example, no seasons to speak of in Los Angeles, and almost any European flower can be grown there at any time of the year; the time of the old world is infinitely rearrangable, in any combination one might prefer.

These are some of the senses in which one may suggest that one sees Los Angeles specifically, or the contemporary (ie, techno-capitalist) world in general, in the Disney Concert Hall. It is at one with some crucial elements of the local concept of the subject, which is an ideal form of the international contemporary subject—multicultural, mobile, sealed off from the sociality of the street by the car or, in older cities that still have populated pavements, the telephone or walkman. (Jogging with a walkman is the ambulatory sped up and simultaneously converted into a private function, subdividing public space between the trajectories of noncommunicating bodies, place incidental to movement, or to an idea of terrain rather than locale.)

But the Disney Concert Hall is a work of art, and as such a combination of what Deleuze and Guattari call 'conceptual personae' and 'aesthetic figures', both of which are 'irreducible to psychosocial types, [and] even if... there are constant penetrations... [i]t seems to us that a social field comprises structures and functions, but this does not tell us very much directly about particular movements that affect the Socius'.[24] By 'conceptual personae' Deleuze and Guattari mean something like embodied ideas, ie, not the philosopher but the philosopher's thinking as a force, whereas they divide 'aesthetic figures' into 'percepts' and 'affects', as follows:

> The difference between conceptual personae and aesthetic figures consists first of all in this: the former are the powers of concepts, and the latter are the powers of affects and percepts. The former take effect on a plane of immanence that is an image of Thought-Being (noumenon), and the latter... on a plane of composition as image of a Universe (phenomenon)... Figures have nothing to do with resemblance or rhetoric but are the condition under which the arts produce affects of

stone and metal, of strings and wind, of line and colour, on a plane of composition of a universe. Art and philosophy crosscut the chaos and confront it, but... [in] the one there is the constellation of a universe of affects and percepts; and in the other, constitutions of immanence or concepts. Art thinks no less than philosophy, but it thinks through affects and percepts.[25]

In practice, as they themselves make clear, works of art never escape philosophy, nor the conceptual the aesthetic, but are combinations of the noumenal and the phenomenal. Seen in these terms, the Disney Concert Hall becomes more obviously about music. The listener is not (only) a social or psychological type, but a body thinking the world through hearing, being in time through, because with, the music.

I propose to describe the programme as the place of the conceptual in the Disney Concert Hall. That is where one finds philosophy, as the logic of form in response to a function. The metal cladding is the aesthetic figure— within the context of a larger one made of the disjunctive interpenetration between the Hall and the rest of the site, where discontinuity and continuity separate and link the stone from and to the metal on the one hand, and the site and the stone-clad buildings around it on the other.

The metal is made of affects that follow from its being metallic: shiny, light-filled and therefore registering lightness, hard, thin. The affects seem to belong to the idea of substance in this formulation, and—with the possible exception of lightness, weight and weightlessness being attributes or associations that inflect space but are not clearly of it—to be exclusively spatial. The percepts belong to movement, and therefore to time at least as much as space: the metal curves and is about slowing down and speeding up. One could also say that affects belong to shape and percepts to surface without shape. (In Bilbao, movements readjust shape by carving volume out of planes that intersect it on different trajectories and at various speeds.)

As one approaches the entrance, then, one is led between curving movements occurring within and across and because of light-filled metal planes. The task of the building is to provide a passage from the visual to the auditory, and it is through its use of percepts that it makes the former introduce the latter and transfer the listener from one to the other at the appropriate moment (fig 36). Movement percepts are linked to spatial affects at first through metal, reflective and weightless (also thin and impenetrable, ie, a surface), as noted, in two stages. The faster horizontal movements of the metal as it extends towards and follows the street, give way to the slower movements that surround the Hall's core, but are then, within the auditorium, transferred from the spatial to the auditory. This is the meaning of the auditorium's symmetry. Outside the building, surfaces made of curves (when considered spatially), or curving surfaces (when considered as movements within contexts of movements, ie, as singular convergences of

Fig. 36   Frank Gehry & Associates: Walt Disney Concert Hall, Los Angeles, 1987–2003, final design model. Photo: Whit Preston, 1999 © FOG&A

movements), combine to make an assemblage of self-supporting surfaces. Each curving in more than one direction at a time, these surfaces join within themselves many movements, and are for that reason not so much de-centred as places of many centres. The cropped, inverted cone to the right of the stairs is the simplest shape, but also one of the most dramatic folds, following a path along the street to the stairs, but then turning away from them, and always angled upwards. (The entrance shows the building divided, beyond the metal another kind of structure, in which there are horizontals and verticals.) Once inside the auditorium, the role of the affects changes completely and percepts cease to be a property of the visual altogether. Singularity gives way to symmetry and repetition (and colour is absorbent rather than reflective). The stage is set for percepts to become entirely a matter of sound. It has been set by way of an exterior that converted form into movement, and now passes that movement back to another form. The passage into the building is: horizontal movement (where affect and percept are equally active); vertical movement (where movement in fact recedes briefly in favour of shape, percepts in favour of affects); invisible movement (movement without gravity save that of the body that hears it as music), where there are only percepts, and affects have to be deduced by the listener, surrounded by other listeners, communally suspended in a private condition facilitated by a programme designed for, or around, sound.

This listener, seated but only apparently disengaged from movement, is anybody as any body, with a continuous and therefore curving skin and at least several centres, which, when enveloped by music—whether in the car or the concert hall—dissolve or disperse into non-spatial (but thought and played and thus material) disembodiments and re-embodiments whose volumes and shapes they occupy (absorb) and whose movements occupy (dissolve) them: 'Concretely, if you define bodies and thoughts as capacities for affecting and being affected, many things change'.[26] Music is time experienced through and in time—as architecture is space experienced as itself reformed—its movements, because disembodied, capable of describing or inventing any body whatsoever.

The body can't close itself to music as easily as it can shut its eyes in front of a painting (one does not have the option of not listening—space gives choices but sound does not). But there's nothing to touch or to see, no inside or outside—and, unlike art made out of words, no flirtation with the unintended or (its opposite) the double entendre, which can use accident to release a meaning one didn't mean to release or to posit an ambiguity. In music, one may use accident to produce meaning, as in any art, but it will not be heard as releasing something otherwise repressed (after all, there's no inside). On the contrary, '[W]e interpret music as the immediate language of the will, and our imaginations are stimulated to embody that immaterial world, which speaks to us with lively motion and yet remains invisible', as Nietzsche put it while still keen on Wagner.[27]

The musical body is the immaterial embodied as invisible movements (percepts) whose relationship to ideas (conceptual personae) is at once clear and uncertain. The immediate language of the will goes in all directions but is nonrepresentational. Nietzsche repeats Schopenhauer's assertion that '[W]hoever gives himself up entirely to the impression of a symphony seems to see all the possible events of life and the world take place in himself. Nevertheless, upon reflection he can find no likeness between the music and the things that have passed before his mind'.[28]

Here, the body finds itself within that which is ordered but is not a language in the sense that it has no equivalent for the semantic, no vocabulary of signifiers for agreed and thus stabilised conceptual signifieds— where, therefore, conceptual personae are at the mercy of aesthetic figures. There can be no etymological dictionary of sounds, hence in part, music's irreducibility to the psychosocial, but the latter would re-emerge in it in the recognition of material things. Schopenhauer explicitly, and Nietzsche implicitly, invoke the symphony. A Deleuzian application of their idea of the body finding itself in the immaterial might want to take account of the presence in the orchestra of recognisable sources for every sound—the cellos are doing this and the French horns that, all in both combination and succession, forming a body of differences combined in a heterogeneous event that is at once a whole. Among the things that might be involved in thinking about the Disney Concert Hall is the notion that nowadays one listens to symphonic music in a world where very little except musical instruments is made of brass and deeply burnished wood, as many of the things in Adolf Loos' house would have been. All sorts of things that were have disappeared, replaced by an electronic world and its own devices. At the auditory level too, recognition in music is now of two kinds. There are sounds made by recognisable instruments, which belong to the world of the pre-electronic, and in most instances even to the pre-industrial, and sounds that are of the electronic era and in that sense continuous with the world at large.

Music is made out of present and past sounds, and the Deleuzian body is an economy of opportunities that makes itself out of any movement it can use. A body never at rest and tied to no necessarily skeletal model—as is also true of music, which, being made out of time, knows the suspension of movement but not its absence (when it's absent the music's over). Music, like the freeway, knows only slow and fast (and anticipation and evocation and echo), while also being a form—like writing and painting (and psychoanalysis), and unlike architecture and sculpture (and anatomy)—in which the inside and the outside coincide as simultaneities, therefore sharing a surface. In the performance of music, mute affect provides the terms for the extraspatial movements that precede it (as conceptual personae) and come with it (as percepts) in the music itself. Hence the need for an idea of surface that first dissolves form and then withdraws itself in the Disney Concert Hall.

Clearly the product of a contemporary grasp of experience—that is to say, of a situation in which the body is more than one thing—the Disney Concert Hall raises the question of what it might be for architecture—an emphatically material art form—to embody musicality. Providing a context for performances doesn't have to mean that one will be struck by the musicality of the building, one might be struck by something else—its use of the technological or the Arcadian, for example. In the case of the Disney Concert Hall, however, one is struck by it. The building itself is most usefully and obviously thinkable in terms of the musical.

Notes

1. Warren Olney, 'Which Way LA?', *KCRW*, Santa Monica, 8 August 1997.
2. Michael Podro, *The Critical Historians of Art*, Yale University Press, New Haven, 1982, p 47.
3. Ibid, p 48.
4. Ibid, p 49.
5. Ibid.
6. Mark Wigley, *White Walls, Designer Dresses: The Fashioning of Modern Architecture*, MIT Press, Cambridge, Mass, 1995.

7. Kirsten Harries, *The Ethical Function of Architecture*, MIT Press , Cambridge, Mass, 1977, p 10.
8. Harries, op cit, p 316.
9. Ibid, pp 316–319.
10. Ibid, p 137.
11. Ibid, p 37.
12. Ibid.
13. Ibid, p 38.
14. Ibid.
15. Wigley, *White Walls*, p 341.
16. Ibid, p 342.
17. See Jeremy Gilbert-Rolfe, 'Blankness as a Signifier', *Critical Inquiry*, XXIV, 1, Autumn 1997, p 165 et passim.
18. Jean Baudrillard in conversation with the author.
19. Gilles Deleuze, *The Fold, Leibniz and the Baroque*, trans Tom Conley, University of Minnesota Press, (Minneapolis, Min), 1977/1987.
20. Gilbert Rolfe, op cit, p 162 et passim.
21. Wigley, op cit, p 14.
22. See, for example, my essay on the bikini as a garment offering a (counter-)critical alternative to piety disguised as social realism: 'The Beach Party and the Parties of Power: Summer's Content, Winter's Discontent', *Beyond Piety, Essays in Art Criticism 1986–1993*, Cambridge University Press, New York, 1995, pp 271–78.
23. TJ Clark, *The Painting of Modern Life, Paris in the Art of Manet and his Followers*, Alfred A Knopf, Inc, New York, 1984, Chapter 2, 'Olympia's Choice', see especially pp 119–46. The chapter concludes (p 146): 'It follows that nakedness is a strong sign of class, a dangerous instance of it. And thus the critics' reaction [to *Olympia*] in 1865 becomes more comprehensible... [However, t]he naked body did without them in the end and did its own narrating. If it could have been seen what signs were used in the process—if they could have been kept apart from the body's whole effect—they might still have been made the critic's property. They would have been turned into objects of play, metaphor, irony, and finally tolerance. Art criticism might have begun'. Clark's invocation of a body that goes its own way and of a modernism unable to concentrate or otherwise deploy nakedness ideologically could be taken as a description of a body that cuts across, or escapes, modernist pathos. Manet's *Olympia* is in this the outer limit of an affirmative negation, and as such, could be said to set the stage for Matisse: affirmation that negates—or is indifferent to—negation.
24. Deleuze and Guattari, *What is Philosophy?*, trans Graham Burchell and Hugh Tomlinson, Verso, London, 1994, p 67.
25. Ibid, pp 65–66.

26. Gilles Deleuze, *Spinoza, Practical Philosophy*, trans Robre Hurley, City Lights Press, San Francisco, 1988, p 124.

27. Friedrich Nietzsche, 'The Birth of Tragedy', *The Birth of Tragedy and the Genealogy of Morals*, trans Francis Golffing, Anchor Books, New York, 1956, p 101.

28. Nietzsche, op cit, p 99.

CHAPTER 4
CONCLUSION:
The Practicality of Planes Taking Flight in Mass, Towards Colour

I do stop, because I am a pragmatic guy and I know I won't get anything built if I don't stop ... Mine are really on budget.

One would have to be truly indifferent to the visual as a source of pleasure—as opposed, for instance, to one of indignation—not to see that the Guggenheim Museum in Bilbao is a great event—of structure and lightness, mass and movement (fig 37). It fits into the city perfectly while being quite unlike it, confirming that Berlin's fear was groundless; and like the Disney Concert Hall it is filled with, or made out of, movement. On first sight, I thought it like seeing major works while a child, when one is able to recognise something as powerful without knowing anything about it. Others have also immediately identified it as a definitive work of contemporary architecture. One has no difficulty reconciling the affective with the cognitive response.

Fig. 37 Frank Gehry & Associates: Guggenheim Museum, Bilbao, Spain Photo: David Heald Copyright SRDF, NY, 1997

Like the Museum Island complex, the Bilbao Guggenheim is adjacent to a river with a bridge going over it that could recall that in which the S-Bahn runs between the Bode and the other museums. One of the things I got excited about when I first saw Gehry's work at a show organised by Lindsey Stamm Shapiro at PS1 in New York in 1977, was how much he fits into the site. Almost all his projects demonstrate this—the Disney Hall being a particularly good example, as is the Loyola Law School project (1981), also in Los Angeles. In Bilbao, the building runs up to and under the bridge (fig 38), becoming progressively more animated as it does so, activating the site while leaving plenty of room for a digressive walk around the outside of the museum.

This can include a climb to a viewing platform, on which one may see from another perspective how the Guggenheim rises above the city, but from a lower starting point than most of it—closer to the boats than to the buildings (fig 39). The museum's own relationship to ships as theme or image is overt (fig 40) but, especially when seen in conjunction with the conventionally rectilinear buildings around it, its use of curvature encourages one to compare it also to the landscape on which Bilbao's other

Fig. 38 Frank Gehry & Associates: Guggenheim Museum, Bilbao, Spain Photo: David Heald Copyright SRDF, NY, 1997

Fig. 39 Frank Gehry & Associates: Guggenheim Museum, Bilbao, Spain Photo: David Heald
Copyright SRDF, NY, 1997

Fig. 40 Frank Gehry & Associates: Guggenheim Museum, Bilbao, Spain Photo: David Heald
Copyright SRDF, NY, 1997

buildings sit. From some views it seems to echo not the architecture around it so much as the topography and urban idea, the piling effect of houses clustered together on hills. Sitting on a slab (like the Disney Concert Hall) the museum rises from the river's edge to fit into the city as the city has fit itself into the hills.

It is a complex building, united by an almost continuous skin that holds together volumes experienced as the products of curving and intersecting planes. The part closest to the street is painted blue, its plaster surface drawing it closer to the buildings on the other side of the street, but the main impression is of silver—especially if one approaches it from a side street, when one encounters it as a huge shining form cropped at the left, right and bottom, clearly large but of an as yet uncertain extensiveness. Once closer, one sees similarities with other Gehry buildings: some details, specifically those having to do with its use of curvature to move upwards, recall the National Nederland building (fig 35, above). Viewed from the front, there are some affinities between the large central forms of the museum and those of the Disney Concert Hall as seen from the entrance (fig 32, above), particularly in the way they are levelled off, but the effect created is not the same because volume is handled so differently in the Bilbao Guggenheim. And from across the river there seems to be some comparison between its lateral movement and that of the Disney Concert Hall along Grand Avenue. These are not very strong similarities, but they are strong enough to remind one that the Disney Concert Hall came both before and after Bilbao. (Another is the echo, in the stone end of the Bilbao Guggenheim, near the car park and containing the front and rear entrances, of the stepped look of early versions of the Disney Hall, eg figs 22, 25, 26, above).

While making notes about the building and its site, I listed its material properties, either individually or in the combinations in which I was seeing them used, ie, as sensations of surface and volume: silver, glass and metal, blue, stone, steam (courtesy of Yves Klein's sculpture) and water. The interior contains white columns, which are not simply vertical (fig 41), and plenty of glass, which is also not presented in terms of right angles. It seemed to me that one couldn't get lost in it but one could get disorientated by it, which potential for inducing confusion I shall describe here as a product and expression of the programme's intention to provide an appropriate space for exhibitions of contemporary art. In order to make that argument, however, I must first expand upon my impressions of the exterior, mostly made of silver material and linked to the water by way of glass and stone, as it is conceptually to the town through blue, the Basque colour of choice.

The titanium, although a metal, with metal's associations of density and strength, advertises its identity as surface rather than support—as a silvery surface sucking in light rather than as steel, to extend the alliteration. It has been manipulated almost like paper, causing the museum to be covered with traces of the hand, like the faint finger- and thumbprints that mark a piece

Fig. 41 Frank Gehry & Associates: Guggenheim Museum, Bilbao, Spain Photo: David Heald
Copyright SRDF, NY, 1997

of pottery's final kneading into its finished form. This also means that walls that read as continuous surfaces from a distance are seen to be less homogeneous when one is close to them, and that the panels glitter even more than if they were perfectly smooth. One's impression is therefore of something like walls made out of light, realising the idea of free-standing immateriality discussed in the last chapter, but achieving this differently here from in the Disney Hall—the distinction being one between continuity in Bilbao versus a relative interruptedness in the Los Angeles building.

Gehry's interest in Gothic architecture leaks into this building—on seeing it, my first thought was of Notre Dame but, as explained, for reasons personally rather than architecturally historical. However, the Gothic is fairly curvy, and about getting mass to ascend, and I've heard Gehry commenting on the thickness of mediaeval walls (and the refined but broad carving of the sculpted figures who live in niches in them), particularly in relation to carved folds and pleats. Gehry's post-medievalism recalls the thick wall in order to present it as hollowed out, while the rest of the programme's elements are designed to undermine or otherwise qualify the image of heaviness that comes with them. In its very complex presentation of this image of massive hollowness, attached to that of lightness by the titanium, this building should be seen as a culmination of a sort, bringing to a new plateau of achievement an architectural practice long identified with animating volumes rather than emphasising weightiness—with making materials true to an image and programme rather than to some idea of themselves. The Bilbao Guggenheim presents the idea of massiveness, and with it the idea of thickness, through the context of very thin cladding and a surface that reflects light. It makes one think that if they could have built the cathedrals out of silver stones, they wouldn't have had to paint them white as Le Corbusier said they did. Which is another way of saying that Gehry has found a way to make the skin of the building less materially emphatic, or perhaps only no more so than the glass that punctuates it.

This is in part because the glass reads as hard, while the titanium is seen to be malleable, in part because where there is glass there is a great deal of activity—concentrated subdivisions or accumulations of movement. It is also because the cladding's thinness contributes to the impression that one is looking at hollow volumes made out of coincident but independent planes, at least as thin as a sheet of glass. I would argue that in this building, glass stands halfway between the titanium and the stone cladding as a sign of solidity, and not, as would usually be the case, as the least dense material on offer on account of its fragility, which is here made to give way to its weight. (The mediaeval too sought to give glass the weight of walls—unfortunately, too often accidentally giving it more.)

In contrast to the thin skin of the forms perceived, due to the metal's luminosity and the movement out of which they are made massive but not ponderous, glass qualifies and adjusts the main directions of forms.

Sometimes it achieves this not by interrupting the plane with which it is generally continuous, so much as by temporarily restating it in terms that include replacing opacity with transparency. More often, it interrupts it—glass making a shape, surface describing a volume—with a movement that contrasts with those around it as it brings the interior into a closer proximity with the outside (fig 42).

In keeping with this emphasis on glass as a surface, panes are not necessarily supported by frames—much of the glass surrounding the elevator shaft, for example, is held in place by magnetic clamps. To all the other things that maintain an air of the active rather than the inert in the building as a whole, one would want to add the presence of provisionality as a sign: outside, titanium plates applied by hand and easily replaceable; inside, a column of cascading, suspended, glass surfaces held in place by magnets.

If stone, titanium and glass represent degrees of light and reflection, the blue part of the Bilbao Guggenheim invokes the same themes by being the colour of water or the sky. However, painting this part of the building blue was not part of the original plan, which was to clad it in titanium. Then someone decided that money could be saved if less titanium were used, and it was agreed that this (administrative) part of the museum would be plastered instead—as noted, it is the part closest to the street and the plastered buildings on it. Nor was the colour, iconographically associated with the region, Gehry's first choice. Possibly he felt some subliminal resistance on the grounds that it was too obvious a thing to do, like painting the Irish Parliament green. In the last chapter, Harries made fun of Semper's emphasis on hygienic association, while Podro quoted his reference to the decorated fabric as the authentic representation of the wall. One supposes that Semper might have come to blue sooner than Gehry, and I think this is because Gehry's work throws any idea of representing and authenticity into a kind of confusion unimaginable to the earlier architect. They tried white first—the Le Corbusier solution—and the building disappeared. Then they tried black, but that was too sombre—bear in mind that this was not the shiny black cube in the Berlin project. Thomas Krens, director of all the Guggenheim museums, wanted to try Cherokee Red, Frank Lloyd Wright's trademark colour and thus an association with the New York building. This didn't work either. At last, encouraged by the Basques, they turned to blue. It remains unclear whether painting the building four times was cheaper than covering it with titanium (figs 43, 44).

However fortuitously then, Gehry has linked the museum to the town through a colour that, in the case of water, describes a surface inseparable from a depth or which, when referring to the sky, evokes the only thing we know that has no surface, and is only depth. If one stands at the site's periphery, the blue element brings together, through a term common to neither, the airiness of the titanium and the rectilinearity of the stone parts of the building.

Fig. 42 Frank Gehry & Associates: Guggenheim Museum, Bilbao, Spain Photo Copyright: Christian Richters, 1997

Fig. 43 Frank Gehry & Associates: Guggenheim Museum, Bilbao, Spain Photo: David Heald Copyright SRDF, NY, 1997

Fig. 44 Frank Gehry & Associates: Guggenheim Museum, Bilbao, Spain Photo Copyright: Christian Richters, 1997

Stone as cladding becomes equivalent to the titanium—an exact match between the traditional and the absolutely new, and the use of a solid as a surface. As noted in Chapter 1, the museum uses local stone, which association attributes another (immaterial) kind of weight to it. As an ornamental symbol with a meaning founded in its indexical relationship to the locale, stone in Bilbao recalls the argument about ideas of permanence in that it reminds one that one may build walls out of anything, but front steps are usually stone. Here, it's much more than the front steps. One can see how Gehry stretched the quarry to the limit. The local stone that surrounds the building outside and clads some parts of its interior as well, connects the outside to the inside as much as glass does. As in the Disney Concert Hall, metal is a feature of the outside exclusively, here giving way on the inside to the white of gallery walls: metal runs continuously from roof to ground, stone from ground or floor to wall; Bilbao stone in tension with international titanium on the outside, and international art-gallery white inside. And stone, while pre-eminently a solid, seemed to me the surface that led most directly to the immediately adjacent conditions of liquidity and the gaseous—the river and the Yves Klein piece that pours steam out from the waterline near the back door, blurring the distinction between water and air. Bilbao is surely as much about the river as anything, founded on water as much as stone. The symbolic order is of stone and fluidity. This is the order Gehry reconvenes in stone and titanium.

My instinct, then, was to describe the building to myself primarily as surfaces, and then compare the most obviously solid of them to liquidity and (accelerated) evaporation (the three conditions of water in relation to heat: stasis, flow, flight as molecular dispersal). The rectilinear is similarly transformed as stone gives way to titanium. Considered as a bundle or pile of movements, verticality of a simple up and down sort is progressively overwhelmed by different sorts of climbing curvature as the building moves towards the bridge. The museum responds to the bridge, making it the measure of how fully it fills the site. One big window runs up against it, while nearby, the building becomes a long gallery that runs underneath it.

What happens in the course of the Bilbao Guggenheim's departure from rectilinearity is the opposite of what metal does in the Disney Concert Hall. There, planes dissolved volumes in the course of expanding and complicating them. Here, surface describes volume, identifying its skin closely with its mass and shape.

As was suggested in Chapter 3, planes in the Bilbao Guggenheim produce volumes that are intact rather than fragmented—one result of which is that edges appear as linear movements that are picked up by the leading in the windows. One's principal impression, though, is of an assemblage of piling and twisting hollow volumes, each created by convergences of independently directed planes that surround and describe it. The hollowness communicated by these volumes is a product of one's perception of the metal as a thin surface that pulls the interior towards the outside, its pale colour and reflexivity concentrating attention on the metal's thinness at the expense of any idea of density. However, in emphasising plane, lightness and mobility also magnify one's sense of the voids they enfold (lightness here being able to reinforce hollowness because it has been associated with the opposite of density). The ensuing semi-autonomy of planes from form, in which they are digressively ascending or laterally extending movements, enclosing, but not restricted to, the solids they describe, causes one's attention to be always moving between surfaces and volumes, the latter destabilised by the animation the former contributes to them.

Gehry uses movement to erode form while depending on other properties to assert it. Writing about him in the 1980s, I said that what seemed at first a formalism of formlessness was more precisely architecture made out of the presentation of multiplicities.[1] In it, form gives way to movements, especially to those describable as digression—movement recognisable as a departure from a path—difference—oscillation between both opposed and sympathetic movements—and meandering—a movement slowed down by seeming to temporarily digress or contradict itself. However, movement animates but does not completely dissolve form in Gehry's architecture. Instead, it makes it ungraspable, which is Kant's primary definition of the sublime. Mass and shape are eroded but not erased by movement's formlessness, hence the architecture's access to the sculptural—which is also animal and gestural—attributes listed by Deleuze and Guattari in the passage quoted above on pages 6 and 7.

Kurt Forster was probably the first to describe Gehry's architecture as sculptural, and he saw it as a sculpture made of the architect's bodily movements: '[M]y spontaneous reaction to [Gehry's buildings] is a curious equivalent to the bodily actions that the artist employs to shape them'.[2] It is, perhaps, but a small step from a body that shapes to a body that thinks itself through movement as much as shape. Both shape and movement have a relationship to gravity that involves an alternation of affirmation and denial—the body thinks of itself as gravitationally bound but of its thinking as unbounded by either of the connotations of gravity. To use a Derridian concept, shape and movement have a differential relationship to one another. Each operates within the terms of the other: shape shapes movements and movements move shapes. Gehry moves shape through three dimensions—depth in any case always hovering over the ideal condition of flatness or two dimensions because materiality brings density (solid, liquid or gas) to it. He does this in two ways at once: up and down, and across, but always through space where the (titanium, glass or stone) surface describes a shape that ends but does not conclude when it meets other shapes or the ground or the air, because it is a singularity made out of only two edges, and therefore a plane. The surface moves in and out of space as it moves through and around it, stopping and starting (or continuing as implication, ie, as fold) around volumes described by the surface as a continuum that curves or bends sharply at will, its edges now interruptions that defer rather than determining. Kept apart, these two movements animate each other. Neither has the last word. As the building moves upwards and away from the car-park and entrances, titanium and reflexivity help the parts of the structure that are most shiny and curvy to seem as though carved from a block of air. Their capacity to do so, however, is predicated on sustaining two incommensurable movements (figs 45, 46).

Inside the building, curvature continues to dictate horizontal as well as vertical movement, and walls and doors aside, there are no, or very few, vertical surfaces. Even in the elevator, one moves vertically through a column that curves, a glass shaft whose form traces a slower movement than one's own. From within an elevator car that is moving vertically, one looks into the museum's central hall, where everything is made of movements that are not at right angles to one another, through a glass screen that traces a movement reminiscent of the building as seen from outside, verticality articulated through ascending curves. This is why I say that one could not get lost but one could become disorientated, which leads to other possibilities for disorientation, including the possibility resident in the question of whether the architecture overwhelms the art or not.

With regard to that question, Gehry relates an anecdote about a conversation he had with Daniel Buren and Michael Asher, back in the 1970s, in which he suggested that artists would prefer exhibition spaces that were self-effacing, only to be surprised at the vehemence with which both rejected the idea, insisting instead that they wanted exhibition spaces that were major works of architecture. (I was told a similar story about Isaac Stern, who during the discussion around the Disney Concert Hall, in which he will play, said that a great hall 'lifts the performers up'.) Should the fact that Asher and Buren are in the business of drawing attention to the spaces in which they install their work seem to render their opinions less than representative, one could turn to Robert Rauschenberg, who, when asked whether the Bilbao Guggenheim threatened to overwhelm what it contained, is reported to have said that were that so it would only mean that artists would have to make better art. He was one of the first to exhibit in it, with an enormous work to which he has been adding for two decades, and in truth, one was not sure whether it was dwarfed or not. Which is to say that one was not sure how good it was.

Rauschenberg is surely right. But the question of whether the building's brilliance undermines what it contains is not the right question in the first place. This is because it should be seen as an introduction to the art presented in it as much as its accompaniment. I mean by this that many things happen to one's habitual relationship to constructed space in the course of seeing the building and then entering it. The rectilinear has been temporarily withdrawn, so that by the time one gets to see a painting,

Fig. 45 Frank Gehry & Associates: Guggenheim Museum, Bilbao, Spain Photo: David Heald Copyright SRDF, NY, 1997

Fig. 46 Frank Gehry & Associates: Guggenheim Museum, Bilbao, Spain Photo Copyright: Jeff Goldberg / Esto

inexorably horizontal and vertical in at least a general sense, one may have taken advantage of the opportunity provided by the architecture to suspend one's habitual relationship to those co-ordinates and get ready to think about such things differently, and certainly more consciously, than usual. The building is challenging to art works, but this has nothing to do with scale or the geometrical irregularity of the main exhibition space. It concerns a more fundamental question of force.

Only works that are forceful, which certainly need not mean large or bright or otherwise loud, could make a proper use of the building, which suggests that it may be hard on minor works for the same reason that it would be the best possible place for major ones. Works of art always have at least to look better than what's already on the street, or else there's no point in going out of one's way to see them. It is not true that they are enhanced by being framed by dullness. Rather, they are best served by being placed in spaces where there is no doubt that they do not have an artificial advantage; but neither should they have an artificial disadvantage. Eisenman's Wexner Center (Ohio State University, Columbus, 1989) might be the kind of architectural challenge to which works of art do not respond well. Perhaps confirming a remark made by Derrida about Eisenman's application of deconstructive thinking being a 'little negativistic',[3] the Wexner Center's desire to make one conscious that it is critically aware of itself gets in the way of the art. Art placed within that variety of criticality doesn't stand a chance, becoming merely a footnote to a discourse—a chorus of conceptual personae—which precludes the aesthetic before it can begin. Gehry, on the other hand, is all percept and affect, maintaining an atmosphere of destabilisation that can correspond to, interact with, and be differentiated from, the singularities of stability and movement reconvened in other terms by the paintings and sculptures it contains. Gehry seems to get more out of dissolving the grid in the interests of the programme, that is to say, than Eisenman does from making architecture that is about exposing it. If you dissolve it then you've dissolved an idea and replaced it with tangibilities, forces that may reflect or contain it but need not be tied to it. If you expose it, all you've done is make an idea into a thing.

Gehry's work has always been about materials as appearance and movement rather than things—ie, about those aspects of things that exceed them as the thing itself exceeds the drawing of it—which is why his architecture is always more than a structure. As a structure that is not only that because it is architecture, therefore symbolically active and as such a symbology using a structure, perhaps its ectoplasmic form could be seen to have the following genealogy, which, if far fetched, nonetheless clarifies Gehry's relationship to the grid, modernism, and the question of the inside's relationship to the outside. If architecture begins with the pyramid, it begins with a form that ascends while burying its interior within a force seen to come from without—the pyramid's sides representing the rays of the sun.

This is replaced with the post and lintel, which reasserts the horizontal while more obviously defying gravity. This, in its turn, gives way to the arch, a line rather than a shape, which parabolically equivocates with gravity—the capstone being a weight that holds things up—and introduces into architecture a support that is a continuous movement rather than a shape, eventually bifurcating into an ascending motion like the pyramid's. Then, add to those three the rectangular steel frame through which modernism finds it possible to make the inside continuous with the outside by extending the grid in the context of as much transparency as possible (for example van der Rohe's Berlin National Gallery, mentioned above). Gehry's work is the next stage, the steel frame liberated from the grid. It is at least possible that he reached this point by confusing grids, making them exceed the idea alleged to govern all of them, and thus forcing them to release the movements they otherwise govern. These would be the other movements of the body, beginning with flow and expansion. If the pyramid represents the rays of the sun, the Bilbao Guggenheim has more to do with the thousand movements of the intransitive body, which is to say that while Gehry's work has never been impassive, now he is able to do more than ever with the skin of the building *as* the building, ie, as the expression and explication of its programme.

This intransitive body never occurs in Gehry's work as representation. The Concord Pavilion may have a science-fiction look, but it doesn't recall a spaceship in the way that Saarinen's TWA terminal at Kennedy Airport recalls a jet aircraft. Likewise, there are points of comparison between the Bilbao Guggenheim and Frank Lloyd Wright's original in New York, beginning with the role of the ectoplasmic in both, and how they fit into their respective sites by standing out. Where Wright's is hemmed in, Gehry's is set back; in the one the grid is interrupted, in the other suspended, both announcing a change of orientation to the spatial by being departures from the rectilinear themselves. In Bilbao and Manhattan, as in Berlin, the museum's relationship to walking plays a part in each case. If Wright imagines a viewer who is slowed down by the building and the art, substituting something more appropriate to contemplation for the less contemplative pace of Fifth Avenue, Gehry, having more space with which to work, has been able to make something where the viewer can wander, a difference no longer of degree but of type.

There is a question here as to whether Gehry's work, if it has become more sculptural, hasn't become so in a way that takes it further from, rather than closer to contemporary sculpture. Gehry has replaced the modernist idea of the cube and the grid with an ectoplasm generated simultaneously from inside and out. Insofar as this describes bodies but not sculptures, it could be that what has been called sculptural in Gehry's work is better considered, in the later but perhaps not in the earlier projects, as having less to do with sculpture than with the figure to which the sculptural may or may not refer. It could be that Gehry's use of the ectoplasm has its origins in

Minimalism, which was after all attacked by Fried for being all surface and no interior articulation (see Chapter 2), but his later work is articulated, precisely on and through its surface rather than in and by its interior, as sculpture rarely, if ever, is. Nonetheless, one would agree with those who call it sculptural in the fundamental sense that it is as unified but animated mass that one first encounters it. Here too, though, one would have to reiterate that this is not a unification or animation one actually sees in contemporary sculpture, where there is less an interaction between both sides of the surface that results in a form, than preservation of the idea of inside and outside by displaying an interior (Judd's boxes open on one side), or by critically obviating it (Lewitt's open cubes made out of line rather than surface). There may be a sculptural equivalent for its animation in Barnett Newman's *Zim Zum* (1969), in which one walks between zigzagging plates, or Serra's *Snake* (1997), for which the latter may provide a precedent, and which was shown at the Bilbao Guggenheim. These too, however, posit an equivalence between inside and outside alien to Gehry, who, as noted, never lets the inside become the negative reflection of the outside. He doesn't deal in repetition in that sense; in his work the inside and outside defer to, but do not repeat, one another.

In his contribution to Der Neue Zollhof development in Dusseldorf, Gehry has begun to thicken the ectoplasm by making it an array of converging planes, which bring the inside out while taking the outside in, compensating for repetition with individuality, each present on a plane that is not reproduced elsewhere in the complex (figs 47–54).

Gehry's Der Neue Zollhof project consists of three buildings, a use of the site he chose so as to provide visual access to the adjacent canal for the people in the buildings behind them—distantly recalling the Concord Pavilion, where he didn't want the building to get in the way of the mountains. Likewise, its use of colour might recall the Experience Music Project, but in this group of office buildings, colour's weightlessness is matched by that of shiny metal in a far more elaborate exchange of equivalences. Surfaces curve, then incidents occur within that curvature that come from elsewhere. But not all the surfaces are curved, nor are any of the buildings alike. Each is a different colour and shape. The rhythm between the buildings changes because of the differences between each of them— determined in their turn by the differences within each—and as it does so, is seen to have to do with compensation and placement. The white and silver buildings having one relationship to the red one, the red and silver another to the white. These triadic relationships are not symmetrical—ie they are not composed of interchangeable terms. White and silver have more in common with each other than either do with red, while silver and red rob surfaces of tangibility in a different way from white—colourless colour of pure form, rather (as is metal) than of ambiguous surface, or (like red) a depth as much as a surface. The plane, in becoming metallic and coloured, already brings

Fig. 47 Frank Gehry & Associates: Neue Zollhof, Dusseldorf, 1995–1999, final design model. Photo: Whit Preston, 1999 © FOG&A

Fig. 48 Frank Gehry & Associates: Neue Zollhof, Dusseldorf, 1995–1999, final design model. Photo: Whit Preston, 1999 © FOG&A

Fig. 49 Frank Gehry & Associates: Neue Zollhof, Dusseldorf, 1995–1999. Photo: Tomaso Bradshaw, 1997 © FOG&A

Fig. 50 Frank Gehry & Associates: Neue Zollhof, Dusseldorf, 1995–1999. Photo: Tomaso Bradshaw, 1997 © FOG&A

Fig. 51   Frank Gehry & Associates: Neue Zollhof, Dusseldorf, 1995–1999. Photo: Tomaso Bradshaw, 1997 © FOG&A

Fig. 52   Frank Gehry & Associates: Neue Zollhof, Dusseldorf, 1995–1999. Photo: Tomaso Bradshaw, 1997 © FOG&A

Fig. 53 (top) Frank Gehry & Associates: Neue Zollhof, Dusseldorf, 1995–1999. Photo: Tomaso Bradshaw, 1997 © FOG&A

Fig. 54 Frank Gehry & Associates: Neue Zollhof, Dusseldorf, 1995–1999. Window Study. Photo: Joshua White, 1996 © FOG&A

with it depth, not as reflection, but as the absence of a certain location for the surface. In conclusion, I want to return to what this does to one's sense not only of what architecture might be—it might be a place that facilitates varied movements by stimulating them—but of what the city might be. Allowing planes to take flight from form through colour or reflexivity or another adventure of the surface—which is what it means to make architecture exceed drawing—returns one to Gehry's thought about democracy being something with which one has an obligation to do something (see Chapter 3).

In Thomas Pynchon's novel *Mason and Dixon* (1997), Dixon points out to Mason that if the world is a sphere then people standing next to one another are actually radiating outwards into space like the spokes on a wheel, their heads fractionally further apart than their feet: 'And wherever you may stand, given the Convexity, each of you is slightly pointed away from everybody else, all the time, out into that Void that most of you seldom notice'.[4] The image is matched by the windows of the Dusseldorf project, which sharing curved surfaces that are not those of spheres, propose an even greater degree and variety of divergences that nonetheless take place next to one another.

Der Neue Zollhof is made of singularities that are once again next to water, in this case a rigidly channelled flow, with which Gehry contrasts a social potential as varied as possible. He designed high rises at the beginning of his career (when he was still working for others); they hold no special challenge for him. They call for and repeat one space, the ideal condition of the absolute grid—which need not actually be present in the street plan but they work best if it is, as New York's Park Avenue confirms. The Dusseldorf project reminds one that in contrast, Gehry proposes a kind of city multitudinous in affect, linked by movements themselves rendered all the more digressive thanks to being channelled through what are explicitly—as it were, by design—singularities. (How different from one another programmes may be within Gehry's practice can be very clearly seen, as has been remarked, by comparing the Museum Island project, which the authorities vetoed, with the bank building they did let him build close by.)

This is the sense in which Gehry's ideas of the social seem to suggest that for him—as for others who have been mentioned here, for example Harries and Wigley, but in terms that I would define as practical rather than theological or ideological—how to live is the art part, and therefore also the ethical part, of architecture. The Dusseldorf project gives people difference as something they may occupy, with exteriors that refuse to be bounded by the grid's finitude. A very new project, the Stata Center at the Massachusetts Institute of Technology (Cambridge, Mass, estimated completion 2003, figs 55, 56), carries Gehry's overloading of the grid to a new level. The scientists who are to occupy it, being themselves quintessentially post-Descartes in their attitudes to grids, love it.

Fig. 55 Frank Gehry & Associates: Stata Center, MIT, Cambridge, Mass., 1998–2004, final design process. Photo: Whit Preston, 2000 © FOG&A

Fig. 56 Frank Gehry & Associates: Stata Center, MIT, Cambridge, Mass., 1998–2004, final design model. Photo: Whit Preston, 2000 © FOG&A

The complexity exploding as singularity in Gehry's later work is the result and expression of what he terms 'richness'. That it is as much a product of social as æsthetic thinking is demonstrated by the direct similarities between the entrances of the Bilbao Guggenheim (fig 57) and the Disney Concert Hall (fig 58). The moment of entry is in each case an event marking the passage from a complex exterior to a space for presenting complexities. It is there that one finds the two sides of Gehry's work most obviously juxtaposed: aesthetically, the entrances are the occasion for dramatic transition between an outside and an inside that relate differentially but not as reflections; socially, they are welcoming and comfortable. One never enters the atrium of a Gehry building to find oneself in a cavern.

Fig. 57 Frank Gehry & Associates: Guggenheim Museum, Bilbao, Spain Photo: David Heald Copyright SRDF, NY, 1997

Fig. 58 Frank Gehry & Associates: Walt Disney Concert Hall, Los Angeles, 1987–2003, final design model. Photo: Whit Preston, 1999 © FOG&A

One finds oneself in the midst of intense activity, which engages but does not overwhelm. In Gehry's practice the idea of the hearth, home, dwelling, or sacred or special place, seems to me to be secularised. I would relate this to the secularisation of beauty as glamour rather than goodness, which is also a characterisation of the contemporary, and which in no sense means the diminution of anything except a disingenuous distrust of the visual.[5] In Gehry's work, this coalesces around the idea of democracy and the need to have something in the building 'interesting to the human'. Gehry is an artist (whether reluctantly or not) who doesn't leave anything to the imagination, in the sense that he prefers instead to create a form made out of the materials and movements of a world ideally composed of more than one system, so that one doesn't predominate, and perhaps too, simply so that one can have more going on. He is prepared to follow the logic of the interesting and good looking, in the course of which (almost) any shape or surface may be combined with any other, providing there's a practical reason for it, which is to say, one that facilitates enjoyment within the terms of the programme.

For example, one can combine stones from Bilbao with titanium, a contrast of surfaces and symbols of the local and the international, and also of stone's archaicism and high technology. This is Heidegger transposed in a way that leads to another question already touched on here with regard to Los

Angeles as a model, which is that of the necessity, in the late twentieth century, for a sense of placelessness as much as of place. In the contemporary world, the international is the local—precisely what Heidegger couldn't stand. It is then, in the international, if anywhere, that the communal would have to be found, in singularity as a property of the city considered as a distinct entity containing every national and cultural type. That is what great cities are, to such a greater extent now than historically as to qualitatively alter everything. In a world where all the shops are the same wherever one goes, all cultural forms are mutations of a ubiquitous displacement.[6]

Gehry plays, affirmatively rather than critically, with what this version of democracy gives him. Speaking of the Guggenheim Bilbao, he told me that 'It should be a pluralist thing because we're talking about democracy; the Colosseum is about democracy'. His notion of architectural democracy is one of infinite adaptability and responsiveness, its opposite something like Robert Stern's Celebration, an American suburban equivalent of Berlin's structural symbolism, and similarly inflexible in its lust for homogeneity. It is ironic that *Der Spiegel* never noticed that Celebration, part of Disneyworld and therefore an extension of the doctrine of conformist fun into everyday life, has strict rules about skylines and property lines and a uniform architectural style, its vulnerability to self-parody suggesting an attitude to urban planning in need of reform if not reinvention. Seeming to have no interest in parody, Gehry proposed neither reform nor reinvention, preferring instead to stick with invention.

Regarding those who inhabit and otherwise use his architecture, there is a final question about Gehry's relationship to the distinction between the organic and the inorganic. Joseph Masheck has suggested that Le Corbusier's description of the house as a 'machine for living', 'may well be a (negative) allusion to Rousseau prompted by a journal entry on man by, of all people, Eugene Delacroix: "that brute... that machine for living, for digestion, and for sleeping"'.[7] As has been said, Gehry makes buildings that facilitate rather than critique. They facilitate a programme designed for inhabitants who define living as neither entirely mechanical nor brutish. And the buildings are, some would say, like their inhabitants, 'machinic assemblies'. This is a term coined by Deleuze and Guattari to describe a process, at once neither and both organic and mechanical, in which one programme is always interfacing with the next in—as in the following example from an essay that applies the term to the question of vision itself—a process of territorialisation, deterritorialisation, and reterritorialisation: 'the mouth, tongue, and teeth "find their primitive territoriality in food" as Deleuze and Guattari put it, and thus are de-territorialised in the production of sound; sounds, in turn, are re-territorialised in meaning'.[8]

I would apply this idea to Gehry's work as follows: the programme as a set of material constraints is the primitive territory of architecture; these are deterritorialised in becoming forms and movements (the symbolic's interface with the material); and reterritorialised in the programme's realisation as architecture, ie, as a place for living. Gehry's idea of the democratic includes a vision of a city opened up and activated by buildings that don't stand still except when you really want them to, for example when you're listening to music or looking at art. Meanwhile, outside, there could be a city composed of singularities instead of repetition, a practical vision that Gehry is always able to bring in on time and to budget.

Notes

1. Jeremy Gilbert-Rolfe, *Beyond Piety: Essays in Art Criticism 1986–1993*, Cambridge University Press, New York, 1995, Chapter 33, 'Intersections', p 334.
2. Ibid, p. 331.
3. Peter Brunette and David Wills, 'The Spatial Arts, an Interview with Jacques Derrida', in Brunette and Wills (eds) *Deconstruction in the visual Arts: Art, Media, Architecture*, Cambridge University Press, Cambridge, 1994, p 27.
4. Thomas Pynchon, *Mason and Dixon*, Henry Holt & Co, New York, 1997. p. 741.
5. For further discussion of the desirability and implications of a secular notion of the beautiful, ie, beauty as glamour rather than goodness, and of a contemporary sublime, found in technology rather than nature, see my *Beauty and the Contemporary Sublime*, Allworth Press, New York, 2000.
6. Attempts to deny this historical reversal are part of contemporary everyday life. American television, for example, unsurprisingly to techno-Capitalism's advantage rather than the reverse, satirically preserves Heidegger's sense of place and rootedness in its own ritualisation of national isolation as authenticity. America television has almost no international news, so that the foreign is kept at a distance at the level of historical fact (information), while being immediately present as consumer fact (infatuation) during advertisements. One is not supposed to know or care what is going on in Germany but one is supposed to want to buy a Volkswagen, partly because it has a foreign name. An American would balk at being offered something called a 'People's Car' in English, feeling that it smacked of an alien ideology.
7. Joseph Masheck, Historical Present: *Essays of the 1970s*, UMI Research Press, Ann Arbor, Michigan, 1984, Chapter 6, 'Corbu in 2-D', p 69.
8. John H Johnston, 'Machinic Vision', *Critical Inquiry*, Autumn 1999, vol 26, 1, p 28.

Index

Alte Nationalgalerie, 31, 53
Altes Museum, 31, 43, 44, 51–52, 56–58,
    60
Altoon, John, 7
American Center, 18, 73, *Fig. 2*, *Fig. 3*
    Use of materials in, 28
Andre, Carl, 5, 40
Asher, Michael, 112

Bacon, Francis, 85
Barron, Stephanie
    'Degenerate Art: The Fate Of The
        Avant–Garde In Nazi Germany',
        Los Angeles
    County Museum of Art, 32
Baudrillard, Jean, 9, 27,
Bauhaus, 29, 47
Berlage, Hendrik, 83, 86–87
Berlin, 47–48, 50–51, 54–55, 56–57, 58,
    60, 63, 69
Bladen, Ronald, 5
Bode Museum, 31, 53
Broad, Eli, 68
Buren, Daniel, 112

California Institute of the Arts, 91
Caro, Anthony, 40
Chiat house (Telluride), 58
Chandler family, 67
Chippendale, David, 39, 46–47
Clark, TJ,
    The Painting of Modern Life, Paris
        in the Art of Manet and his
        Followers, 89, 98
Concord Pavilion, 15–21, 23, 68, 115,
    116, *Fig. 1*
    And movement, 25
    And site, 15–17, 18
    And the landscape, 16, 24, 26
Crystal Cathedral, 27

'Degenerate Art: The Fate Of The Avant–
    Garde In Nazi Germany', Los
    Angeles County
    Museum of Art, 32

Delacroix, Eugene
    On Jean Jacques Rousseau, 126
Deleuze, Gilles and Félix Guattari, 46,
    91, 126
    What is Philosophy?, 6–7, 93–94
Deleuze, Gilles, 3, 7, 51, 60
    Cinema One: the Movement Image,
        59
    Spinoza, Practical Philosophy, 96
    The fold, 59
    The Fold, Leibniz and the Baroque,
        85
    See also Deleuze, Gilles and Félix
        Guattari
Der Spiegel, 48, 49, 54, 126
    On Frank Gehry, 28, 45–46
Derrida, Jacques, 3, 81, 85, 114
DG Bank Building, 48
Dirkson, Everett, 68
Dube, Wolf, 32, 33, 46
Duchamp, Marcel, 85

Eisenman, Peter, 2, 3, 18
    Wexner Center for the Arts, 114
Experience Music Project, 21–25, *Fig 4*,
    Fig 5
    And movement, 22, 25
    Use of colour in, 23–24, 90, 116
Fish,
    Frank Gehry and, 59
Forster, Kurt, 13, 46
    On Frank Gehry, 13, 111
Fried, Michael, 81, 116
    'Art and Objecthood', 39–40

Galeries Lafayette, 55, 56
Gehry house, 4
Gehry, Frank, 1–2, 13
    American Center, 18, 28, 73, *Fig. 2*,
        Fig. 3
    And democracy, 67, 92, 125, 126–127
    And fluidity, 59–60
    And form, 21, 58, 79, 90, 111, 125, 126
    And Los Angeles, 7–9, 26–27, 91–93,
        126

And materials, 1,2, 4, 8, 9, 13,14,
    17–18, 21, 27–28, 53, 58, 73,
    86–87, 90, 110, 114, 125, 127
And Minimalism, 39–40, 43–44
And movement, 26, 43, 54–55, 56,
    58, 91–92, 110–111, 114, 122,
    125, 126
And music, 63, 91–92, 94, 96–97
And Pop Art, 6
And sculpture, 5–6, 14–15, 23, 111,
    115
And site, 3, 15–16, 18, 20–21, 24,
    66–67, 84
And surface, 85–86, 88–89, 91, 110,
    111, 116
And technology, 26
And the grid, 57–58, 69, 84, 92, 114,
    115, 122
Chiat house (Telluride), 58
Concord Pavilion, 15–21, 23–26, 68,
    115, 116, *Fig. 1*
'Degenerate Art: The Fate Of The
    Avant–Garde In Nazi Germany'
    exhibition
design, 32
DG Bank Building, 48
Experience Music Project, 21–22,
    23–24, 25, 90, 116, *Fig 4, Fig 5*
Gehry House, 4
Guggenheim Museum, Bilbao, 1,
    20, 27–28, 57–58, 66, 70, 83, 86,
    90–91, 94, 101–114, 123, 125–126,
    *Fig 37, Fig 38, Fig 39, Fig 40,
    Fig 41, Fig 42, Fig 43, Fig 44,
    Fig 45, Fig 46, Fig 57*
Hollywood Bowl, 68
Interest in Gothic architecture, 106
Liquidity, 59
Loyola Law School, 102
Merriweather Post Pavilion of
Music, 17
Museum Island, 1, 15, 20, 21, 31–62,
    64, 66, 83, 102, *Fig 6, Fig 7,
    Fig 8, Fig 9, Fig 10, Fig 11,
    Fig 12, Fig 13, Fig 14, Fig 16,
    Fig 17, Fig 18, Fig 19*
Nationale–Nederlanden Bank
    Building, 28, 86, 104, *Fig 35*

Neue Zollhof, 70, 116–122, *Fig 47,
    Fig 48, Fig 49, Fig 50, Fig 51,
    Fig 52, Fig 53, Fig 54*
On ornament, 83
On process, 88
Samsung Museum of Modern Art,
    59
Santa Monica Place Mall, 4
Stata Center, Massachusetts
Institute of Technology, 122, *Fig 55,
    Fig 56*
Use of colour, 23–24, 90, 107, 116,
    122
Use of models, 13, 58, 64
Vitra Furniture Museum, 28, 85
Walt Disney Concert Hall, 1, 22, 24,
    26–27, 52, 63–99, 101, 102, 104,
    110, 112, 123, *Fig 20, Fig 21,
    Fig 22, Fig 23, Fig 24, Fig 25,
    Fig 26, Fig 27, Fig 28, Fig 29,
    Fig 30, Fig 31, Fig 32, Fig 33,
    Fig 34, Fig 36, Fig 58*
World Exhibition Amphitheatre, 59
Germany, 48
    Reunification, 50, 60
    See also Berlin
Goldblatt, David,
    On Peter Eisenman, 2
Gothic Architecture, 106
Grassi, Giorgio, 33, 39, 43, 45, 46–47, 53,
    54
Gropius, Walter
    Bauhaus, 29, 47
Grosvenor, Robert, 5
Guattari, Félix, *See Deleuze, Gilles and
    Félix Guattari*
Guggenheim Museum, Bilbao, 1, 20,
    57–58, 70, 86, 101–114, 123,
    125–126, *Fig 37, Fig 38, Fig 39, Fig
    40, Fig 41, Fig 42, Fig 43, Fig 44,
    Fig 45, Fig 46, Fig 57*
    And form, 106–107, 111
    And movement, 91, 94 107, 108, 111
    And site, 102–104,
    And surface, 83, 104–106, 108, 110–112
    Use of colour in, 104, 107
    Use of materials in, 27–28, 90–91,
        104–107

Harries, Karsten, 30,107
  On Walter Gropius and the
    Bauhaus, 29
  The Ethical Function of
    Architecture, 20, 29, 81–83,
Hegel, GWF, 50, 54, 84
  The Philosophy of History, 48
Heidegger, Martin, 3, 8, 18, 24, 26. 58,
    84–85, 89, 90, 125–126
  Poetry, Language, Thought, 25
  The Origin of the Work of Art, 20
  The Question Concerning
    Technology, 25, 28
Hoffman, Ludwig
  Pergamon, 41
Hollein, Hans, 63
Hollywood Bowl, 68

Jameson, Frederic
  Postmodernism, or, The Cultural
    Logic of Late Capitalism, 10–11
Johns, Jasper, 40
Johnston, John
  'Jameson's Hyperspace, Heidegger's
    Rift, Frank Gehry's House', 11
  'Machinic Vision', 126
Judd, Donald, 5, 40, 116

Kant, Immanuel, 3, 84, 111
Kelly, Ellsworth, 40
Koshalek, Richard, 63
Krens, Thomas, 107

Le Corbusier (Charles Édouard Jeanneret),
    63, 82, 84, 85, 89, 106, 107, 126
LeWitt, Sol, 1, 116
Libeskind, Daniel, 61
Lilla, Mark, 10
Loos, Adolph, 82, 89, 97
Los Angeles County Museum of Art, 32,
    66, 67
Los Angeles Times, 67
Los Angeles, 1–2, 7–9, 26–27, 63–99,
    125–126
Louvre, 32, 49
Loyola Law School, 102

Manet, Edouard
  Olympia, 89
Masheck, Joseph, 126
Matisse, Henri, 88
  Red Studio, 23
Merleau–Ponty, Maurice, 18, 56
Merriweather Post Pavilion of Music, 17
Merz, Gerhard and OM Ungers, 31
Messel, Alfred
  Pergamon, 41
Mickey Mouse's head, 9
Mies van der Rohe, Ludwig
  National Gallery, Berlin, 88, 115
Minimalism, 7, 39–40, 43, 116
  And architecture, 5–6
  And music, 63
Modernism, 10, 20, 82–83, 88–90, 114,
    115
Morris, Robert, 5, 40
Museum Island, 1, 15, 20, 21, 31–62, 74,
    76, 83, 102, Fig 6, Fig 7, Fig 8, Fig 9,
    Fig 10, Fig 11, Fig 12, Fig 13, Fig 14,
    Fig 16, Fig 17, Fig 18, Fig 19
  And Berlin, 48
  And movement, 54–55, 56
  Bridge linking Neues and Altes
    Museum, 32, 41, 44–45, 47, 53
  Master plan, 32, 41–44
Muscum of Contemporary Art (MoCA),
    66, 67

Namier, Louis, 20
Nationale–Nederlanden Bank Building,
    28, 86, 104, Fig 35
Neue Zollhof, 116–122, Fig 47, Fig 48,
    Fig 49, Fig 50, Fig 51, Fig 52,
    Fig 53, Fig 54
  And surface, 116
  Windows, 70, 86
Neues Museum, 31, 32, 39, 40–41, 43–44,
    47, 52, 53, 56, 58, 60, Fig 15
New Minimalism, 33, 39–40, 43–44, 47,
    53, 54
Newman, Barnett,
  Zim Zum, 116
Nietzsche, Friedrich, 81, 96

Human, All Too Human, 29–30
Nouvel, Jean, Emmanuel Gattani and
    Associates
    Galeries Lafayette, 55, 56

Oldenberg, Claes, 5, 6

Pergamon, 31, 41, 44, 48, 55–58, 60
Podro, Michael, 80–81, 107
    The Critical Historians of Art, 97
Pop art, 6
Postmodernism, 2
Postmodernists, 2,
Post–Structuralism, 3, 10
Pynchon, Thomas
    Mason and Dixon, 122

Rauschenberg, Robert, 112
Riordan, Richard, 68
Russian Formalism, 3

Saarinen, Eero
    TWA Terminal, 115
Samsung Museum of Modern Art, 59
Santa Monica Place Mall, 4
Schinkel, Karl Friedrick, 41, 53, 55
    Altes Museum, 31, 48
Schopenhauer, Arthur, 96
Sculpture, 7, 14–15, 23, 111, 115
    1960s American, 5–6, 39
Semper, Gottfried, 79–83, 89, 90, 107
Serra, Richard, 5, 6, 7, 39–40
    One Ton Prop (House of Cards), 5
    Snake, 116
Shapiro, Lindsey Stamm, 102
Shklovsky, Viktor, 3
Site, 2, 3–4
Smith, Tony, 40
Stata Center, Massachusetts Institute of
    Technology, 122, *Fig 55, Fig 56*
    And the grid, 122
Stella, Frank
    And minimalism, 43–44
Stern, Issac, 112
Stern, Robert
    Celebration, 126

Stirling, James, 63
Structuralism, 3
Stüler, Frederich August,
    Neues Museum, 41, *Fig 15*

Trollope, Anthony, 61–62

Ungers, Om and Gerhard Merz, 31

Venturi, Robert, 18
Vitra Furniture Museum, 28, 86

Wagner, Richard, 81, 96
Walt Disney Concert Hall, 1, 22, 24, 26,
    52, 63–99, 102, 104, 110, 112, 123,
    Fig 20, Fig 21, Fig 22, Fig 23, Fig 24,
    Fig 25, Fig 26, Fig 27, Fig 28, Fig 29,
    Fig 30, Fig 31, Fig 32, Fig 33, Fig 34,
    Fig 36, Fig 58
    And form, 77–79, 84, 90–91
    And Los Angeles, 91–93
    And movement, 70, 91–92, 94–96,
        101
    And music, 63, 66, 91–92, 94, 96–97
    And site, 73, 76–77, 84
    And surface, 79, 83–86
    And the grid, 69, 76, 92
    Model of, 64
    Use of materials in, 27, 70, 73–74,
        94–96
Wexner Center for the Arts, 114
Wigley, Mark,
    White Walls, Designer Dresses: The
    Fashioning of Modern Architecture,
        81–82, 83, 86, 89–90
Wildung, Dietrich, 32, 44, 45, 46, 47, 51
    On Frank Gehry's Museum Island
    proposal, 31
    On Giorgio Grassi's Museum Island
    proposal, 45
Winckelmann, Johann Joachim, 50
World Exhibition Amphitheatre, 59
Wright, Frank Lloyd, 107
    Guggenheim Museum, New York,
        115